THE MULTI-DIRECTIONAL LEADER

RESPONDING WISELY
to CHALLENGES
from EVERY SIDE

TREVIN WAX

The Multi-Directional Leader:
Responding Wisely to Challenges from Every Side
Copyright © 2021 by Trevin Wax

Published by The Gospel Coalition

The Gospel Coalition
P.O. Box 170346
Austin, Texas 78717

Art Direction: Steven Morales
Cover Design: Matt Mantooth
Typesetting: Ryan Leichty

Unless otherwise indicated, all Scripture quotations are taken from the Christian Standard Bible, Copyright 2017, 2020 by Holman Bible Publishers. Used by permission.

ISBN:
978-1-7334585-8-0 (Print)
978-0-9992843-6-0 (Mobi)
978-0-9992843-5-3 (ePub)

Printed in the United States of America

"Trevin Wax writes with keenness of insight, pastoral wisdom, and prophetic forcefulness. In this book he articulates the pressure today's Christian leaders feel from every direction. Wax remains one of my most reliable counselors for leading in a rapidly shifting context."

J. D. GREEAR, pastor, The Summit Church, Raleigh-Durham, North Carolina; president, Southern Baptist Convention

"Leadership is challenging. It requires wisdom, thoughtfulness, prayerfulness, and humility. It also requires an awareness that a one-size-fits-all leadership approach falls short as a method of engaging with different types of people and situations. As we seek to serve and care for others, we need the compelling vision Trevin Wax offers in his book, *The Multi-Directional Leader*. In whatever ways you lead and influence others—as a CEO, ministry leader, or parent—this book offers insightful questions and commentary to grow as a versatile leader, considering the needs of others as you guide those entrusted to your care."

MELISSA KRUGER, author and director of women's initiatives for The Gospel Coalition

"Calling for Christian leaders in churches, organizations, institutions, and other settings to avoid the shortcomings of a single-perspective approach to leadership, Trevin Wax, in a thoughtful manner informed by Scripture and compelling biographical examples, convincingly shows the importance for leaders to understand people, contexts, issues, and decision-making from a multi-directional perspective. Though intended only as a brief overview, this insightful volume skillfully addresses the complexity of leadership in theory and in practice. Let us pray that the Lord will use this significant resource to raise up a new generation of faithful multi-directional leaders who will selflessly, compassionately, and courageously serve church and society in the days ahead. I am delighted to recommend this timely and applicable book."

DAVID S. DOCKERY, president, International Alliance for Christian Education; Distinguished Professor of Theology, Southwestern Seminary

"They say that generals fight the last war. Indeed, Christian leaders are often fighting their previous battles. All of us fall into cognitive rituals that are comfortable but don't help us to grow, thus limiting our ability to lead. Trevin Wax reminds us of this tendency with a book that will challenge those of us willing to engage in introspection of how we may be one-directional. He writes in a manner that isn't limited by political or theological preferences. Just about anyone in a leadership role can benefit from this book. We in the Christian community are blessed to have such a voice to help position us to be ready for the challenges we face in the 21st century."

GEORGE YANCEY, professor of sociology, Baylor University; author of *Beyond Racial Gridlock*

CONTENTS

PART ONE

MULTI-DIRECTIONAL
LEADERSHIP EXPLAINED

PART TWO

MULTI-DIRECTIONAL
LEADERSHIP APPLIED

For Ivan Mesa

FOREWORD

Jesus said, "I have not come to bring peace, but a sword" (Matt. 10:34, ESV). The apostle Paul wrote of "our warfare" (2 Cor. 10:4). He wanted the early church to "get ready for battle" (1 Cor. 14:8). He called Timothy to accept hardship "as a good soldier of Christ Jesus" (2 Tim. 2:3). Conflict—for the sake of the gospel—is a clearly declared theme in the New Testament.

Because you have picked up this book, I have two hunches about you. On the one hand, you accept that advancing the gospel will at times pull you into worthy conflicts. On the other hand, you reject petty conflicts and selfish controversies as distasteful violations of the gospel. This new book by Trevin Wax will help you grow both in your courage and in your caution.

I am glad that Trevin has written *The Multi-Directional Leader: Responding Wisely to Challenges from Every Side*. We need this book. As we are being buffeted on every side—and I expect it to get worse—staying steady under multiple pressures isn't easy, is it?

Decades ago, Francis Schaeffer taught me something that has helped me through the years. It is the wisdom permeating this book. Here's the insight: *we rarely have the luxury of fighting on one front only*. Christian faithfulness often requires us to fight on two opposite fronts simultaneously. For example, when we take a stand against false doctrine, we must simultaneously take a stand against ugly harshness. We see the monster of heresy in front of us, and we rightly resist the error. But if we are not paying attention, we might not notice the other monster behind us—the brutality of a censorious spirit. We can easily back right into its jaws.

If the challenges coming at us were one-dimensional, or if they came at us sequentially rather than simultaneously, we could stay focused on one problem at a time and press through more easily. But the battle rarely unfolds so simply.

Here is another layer of complication. We import our hypocritical group biases into our conflicts. Our sense of moral urgency rises when we see a failing among our opponents, and our drive for correction relaxes when we see it among our allies.

What's more, each of us has very personal inclinations. By temperament, we are naturally sensitive to some issues even as we are less alert to other truly weighty concerns. For example, some of us are naturally gripped by the standards and definitions and clearly drawn lines of doctrinal truth. Others of us naturally gravitate toward the vibe and feel and tone of warm relationships. We turn God's both-and into our own either-or—without even realizing it.

For all these reasons and others, it can be easy for us to be half-right as we contend for some aspect of the gospel. And because, at that particular point, we really are half-*right*, we do not see that we are also half-*wrong*—or, at least, incomplete. We see and rejoice in the good and true boxes we have rightly checked off. But we honestly do not perceive how many blanks we have never filled in. We can be blind to the towering beauty of fully developed, well-proportioned, mature, biblical Christianity—"the measure of the stature of the fullness of Christ" (Eph. 4:13).

I will make it even worse. Fighting on one front only can reap huge rewards. It is a way to get noticed, create a platform, and generate a following. Just beat the drum loud and long for one facet of a multi-faceted gospel issue. Many people will rally to a church or ministry that specializes in being oh-so-right—in one respect. It gets likes and reposts and mentions and money. And this way of making a name for yourself does not require you to deny the gospel. All you have to do is keep repackaging your one theme within the gospel—rather than undertake the more demanding, more ennobling, more life-giving task of declaring the totality of the biblical gospel, so that the true magnificence of Christ can be seen by more and more people.

Let's all face ourselves honestly about these temptations and pit-falls. But for now, I ask that we notice just the obvious: *a half-fought battle is not a well-fought battle*. Even an apparent victory conceals the actual grandeur of our Lord, in all his grace and all his claims. Fighting a battle on one front only can, and probably will, lose the war.

This is why Trevin's book matters so much. If we will make the vision and the wisdom of this book a matter of ongoing discussion and prayer in our generation, 20 years from now we gospel-loving Christians will be more united together and more compelling to our world. We will have fewer church splits and more church plants, less controversy and more solidarity, quieter hearts, fuller praises, and new conversions to Christ, because our more mature Christianity will be a persuasive and inviting alternative to cross over into.

Wonderfully, our Lord above is for us in this very way. We do not have to hold the full magnitude of the gospel together in our own strength. If we will look to him moment by moment, he will help us transcend ourselves and our limitations and fears and prejudices. And we will, imperfectly but really, represent the glories of Christ with more and more public obviousness, as we grow into the stature of his fullness.

Ray Ortlund
Renewal Ministries
Nashville

INTRODUCTION

THE SHEPHERD AND THE FIELD

Night was falling over the fields when we first heard the pitiful cries—a combination of bleats and squeals coming from somewhere ahead of us. I was on a walk with one of the guys from the youth group in the village church where I ministered every week, a small rural community on the edge of western Romania. The sound signaled that one of the neighbor's sheep was in crisis, perhaps caught in a trap. As we picked up our pace and followed the cries, straining to see in the last light of day, we came upon two wild dogs that had seized a lamb and were tearing into its neck. We grabbed for a stick or rock—anything we could throw—and after we lunged at the dogs, they made a hasty retreat.

A little boy from the village church, Dani, no more than 9 years old, rushed to our side, saw the lamb in distress, and then ran back in tears to his home. The lamb belonged to his family, and he and his older brother were tending the sheep that day.

It was too late for the lamb. Its neck was torn; blood was everywhere. Each time the lamb tried to stand and walk, it could no longer hold its head or control its neck. Collapsing over and over, all it could do was issue those pitiful cries. I was an American from the suburban South, and though I was fluent in Romanian and knew something of the agrarian culture of this and similar villages, I had never been in this situation before. I had no clue how to respond. It was left to the older brother in the family to come over, see the severity of the wounds, and tell us there was nothing more we could do.

———

The New Testament describes God's people as a flock (Luke 12:32; John 10:16) and Jesus as the chief shepherd (1 Pet. 5:4). What an honor for a pastor to be designated the role of undershepherd—the keeper of the flock that remains God's possession, bought with the blood of the Good Shepherd who laid down his life for the sheep (1 Pet. 5:2; John 10:11–13). The heart of a good pastor beats with loving care for Jesus's sheep.

When I come across passages that describe the church as a flock and its leaders as shepherds, I often think back to that night in a Romanian village—recalling that flock, that field, those wild dogs, and that little lamb's fate. It reminds me of the seriousness of shepherding and what's at stake when wolves attack.

We're called to "be on guard" for ourselves and for "all the flock of which the Holy Spirit has appointed" us as overseers, ready to fend off "savage wolves" (Acts 20:28–29). We're called to "shepherd God's flock" (1 Pet. 5:2), feed the lambs who belong to the Lord (John 21:15), and protect them when danger arises (John 10:12). Faithful shepherds remain alert, ready for battle when wolves invade the field. Taking up God's Word as a sword, we fend for the sheep and fight off threats.

Alertness requires the shepherd to remember that dangers creep up on the sheep from multiple directions. Many pastors and church leaders today assume the most dangerous threats to God's people will show up on the edges of only one side of the field. Perhaps we've grown so accustomed to challenges coming from one area that we lose sight of threats appearing from the opposite direction. We fancy ourselves as warriors who protect the sheep, alert to challenges that may arise, but our gaze is ever turned in only one direction—and so we unintentionally leave the sheep vulnerable to different dangers.

This book is for pastors and church leaders, terms I'll use interchangeably because my counsel applies not only to the pastoral role, but also to other Christian leaders in a variety of settings. I'm writing to those who exert influence, whether in the church, or in the academy, or in a Christian organization, or through teaching or writing. Pastors are responsible for the sheep God has entrusted to their care. Leaders are to steward well the people who follow them as they follow Christ (1 Cor. 11:1).

This book exhorts pastors and church leaders toward a vision of leadership I call "multi-directional," which I contrast with the more common (and less effective) "one-directional" leadership. One-directional leaders are skillful in spotting and thwarting threats to the sheep that come from a single direction of the field. But because they focus on fighting battles on one front, they leave the flock vulnerable to problems from other sides. Multi-directional leaders, on the other hand, fend off threats from more than one direction. They hold up Scripture and fearlessly proclaim truths that cut to the root of our sins, failures, and dysfunctions, no matter what political or theological categories are crossed. They don't let fear dictate their theological statements or determine their cultural posture.

To be multi-directional is to lead with dexterity and discipline—a faithful versatility that challenges erroneous positions no matter where they come from, and promotes a full-orbed vision of ministry that defends the truth and protects the flock. This book is about developing this discipline. Our goal is to learn how to better and more effectively respond with wisdom to challenges from every side.

PART ONE

MULTI-DIRECTIONAL LEADERSHIP EXPLAINED

My goal in this section is to explain the concept of multi-directional leadership, first by contrasting it with the more common one-directional leadership. In the first chapter, we look at the multi-directional impulse in various fields: business, parenting, and the day-to-day work of pastoral counseling.

In the next two chapters, we apply the concept to theology and practice. I offer some examples of what multi-directional leadership looks like when theology is contested, and then I give a few examples from Scripture and from church history, focusing primarily on John Stott as a recent example of someone who embodied this value. We look carefully at several ways leaders can cultivate a multi-directional sensibility in ministry.

Many cultural forces both inside and outside the church press against us and make it difficult to become multi-directional leaders. For this reason, in chapter 4, I examine some of the obstacles to multi-directional leadership—challenges that make it more attractive to remain one-directional so as not to invite criticism, rebuke, or controversy. We look at some of the barriers to growing in this skill, as well as the hurdles we have to cross if we hope to remain multi-directional for the duration of our ministries.

1

ONE-DIRECTIONAL VS. MULTI-DIRECTIONAL LEADERSHIP

The burdens of Christian ministry are many. Faithful pastors care for the souls they shepherd. They care also for the Scriptures they are called to teach. They care about the cultural context in which they spread the good news of King Jesus. Good pastors work to preserve the unity of their congregation as they aspire to remain grounded in truth and overflowing in love. These are some of the primary burdens a pastor carries. Other Christian leaders also share in these burdens, even if the scope of responsibility and field of action look different.

Multi-directional leadership—the desire to show faithful versatility in applying the truth of God's Word in today's cultural context—matters most amid conflict, when dangers that threaten the flock are most prevalent. But multi-directional leadership also matters in a general sense. We need this faithful versatility in order to carry several pastoral burdens: the care of souls, commitment to Scripture, and concern for the culture.

CARE OF SOULS

Consider a pastor's care for members of the congregation. In counseling, a one-directional leader will tend to prescribe the same spiritual medicine no matter the ailment. Warnings, admonitions, and exhortations will all sound the same. The one-directional pastor diagnoses a narrow set of spiritual sicknesses, mixes a narrow set of prescriptions, and stays alert to a narrow set of potential dangers.

In contrast, consider Paul's approach in addressing the Thessalonians. He exhorts the family of God to "warn those who are idle, comfort the discouraged, help the weak," and "be patient with everyone" (1 Thess. 5:14)—four different prescriptions. To know when and whom we are to warn, comfort, and help, we need God's wisdom and guidance. We must be versatile in our application.

Paul's instruction doesn't apply only to the pastoral role, of course, as this vision of ministry extends to members of the congregation who care for one another. He assumes this versatility—the wise and discerning application of truth to life—will occur among all church members. Perhaps the lazy person needs a tough warning about spiritual drift, while another believer needs an encouraging word of comfort. The one who is spiritually or physically weak will need others to come alongside and help. In all of these cases, patience is required.

We see in this rapid-fire set of instructions a truth central to multi-directional leadership: different problems require different remedies. Matt Smethurst puts it this way: "Paul is a physician of souls, prescribing different medicines for different maladies, and he expects ordinary church members to do the same."[1] The right counsel at the right time—this is multi-directional leadership in the ordinary work of a pastor or other church leader.

Sometimes, this care for souls is expressed not only through the right word, but the right emphasis. To the woman caught in adultery, Jesus said two things: "Neither do I condemn you. Go, and from now on do not sin anymore" (John 8:11). The tenderhearted person racked with guilt over lingering sin may need the pastor to emphasize Jesus's

---

1.   Matt Smethurst, *1–2 Thessalonians: A 12-Week Study*, Knowing the Bible (Wheaton, IL: Crossway, 2017), 58.

first word of no condemnation; the *comfort* of the gospel is the note to play. But the believer steeped in sin who appeals to cheap grace in order to excuse a heart of indifference may need the pastor to emphasize Jesus's second word, the Spirit-filled command to no longer live in sin; the *challenge* of the gospel is the right note.

Caring for souls requires us to consider the right word, the right prescription, the right emphasis, and the right note at the right time.

COMMITMENT TO SCRIPTURE

In preaching and teaching, pastors and other Christian leaders must learn to handle Scripture with care. When we find complementary truths that at times seem to stand in tension with one another, the multi-directional leader finds such complexity beautiful and doesn't shrink back from declaring the whole counsel of God (Acts 20:27). A one-directional leader, however, often falls back on the same biblical texts, preferring to lean on verses and passages that reaffirm the congregation's assumptions and preconceptions. As a result, some biblical truths are emphasized out of proportion, while other important truths are screened out entirely.

For example, some churches focus on the Christian's responsibility as salt and light in society, but with little emphasis on calling people to personal faith in Jesus. In other churches, congregants are assured every week of their personal salvation and exhorted to pursue individual holiness, but the Christian's social responsibility to the poor and oppressed draws scant attention.

In his second letter to Timothy, Paul warned about the temptation to satisfy itching ears. "People will not tolerate sound doctrine," he wrote, "but according to their own desires, will multiply teachers for themselves because they have an itch to hear what they want to hear" (2 Tim. 4:3). It's easy to read a passage like this and assume the solution is to preach sound doctrine with passion, and this certainly makes sense as one way to apply the text. But a multi-directional leader recognizes many types of itching ears. Ear-tickling preaching can also consist of strong warnings about real doctrinal dangers—as long as your listeners enjoy hearing about problems that threaten everyone else. Your sermon may be a fiery broadside against a legitimate threat, but if you only alert your flock to dangers they've long learned to see clearly, *you* may consider yourself a prophet, when in reality you're just a one-directional dispenser of selective warnings.

CONCERN FOR CULTURE

Church leaders are right to show concern for the cultural context in which we're called to serve. One-directional leaders too often let the culture set the agenda for the subjects a pastor will address. Throughout history, many Christian leaders have settled for a narrow set of topics, a sliver of issues determined not by biblical emphasis but by the enthusiasm of their followers.

Take Billy Sunday, for example—a renowned 20th-century revivalist known for his fiery preaching against various sins of immorality and personal vice. His sermons certainly intended to "engage the culture" of his day. He relished his image as a preacher unafraid to take on people's sins—certain sins, that is. Curiously missing from his litany of evils was the racial injustice of the era that provided cover for the resurgent Ku Klux Klan and led to the Great Migration of black people from the South to the North.

Before Sunday's visit to Washington, DC, in 1918, an African American Presbyterian minister, Francis Grimké, urged him to confront racism. Sunday declined. Reflecting later on the event, Grimké wrote,

> The members of our white churches are now, doubtless, patting themselves on the shoulder, chuckling in their sleeves, congratulating themselves upon the fact that they have passed safely through the ordeal of Mr. Sunday's diatribes, his scathing criticisms and denunciations without once being called to time by him for this sin [of racial prejudice]. . . . No word of condemnation, of disapproval fell from his lips, while denouncing almost every other sin under heaven.[2]

2.   Francis Grimké, "Billy Sunday's Campaign in Washington, D.C.," *The Works of Francis J. Grimké: Volume 1, Addresses Mainly Personal and Racial* (Washington, DC: Associated Publishers, 1942), 555. On a similar note, in 1886 American journalist and activist Ida B. Wells heard D. L. Moody preach. Wells praised Moody for his style and for his presentation of the gospel of Christ crucified for sinners, yet wanted to ask why he accommodated segregation in the South and "never touched upon that phase of sin—caste distinction—practiced even in the churches and among

Tensions over what sins are "respectable" remain with us today. Not long ago, I heard from a pastor on the West Coast who planned to mention the evil of abortion during a time of public prayer and received pushback from members of his staff. They worried some visitors might be offended. He found it interesting that in previous prayer times, no one had questioned his stance on issues related to a Christian's care for immigrants or our country's racial injustice. I've spoken with pastors in the Deep South whose experience has been the opposite. Church members expect the pastor to pray for the abolition of abortion, but grow nervous when prayers focus on the less fortunate, the immigrant, or victims of racial discrimination.

One-directional leaders avoid these moments of tension in one of two ways. Either they claim biblical fidelity requires them to give little thought to their cultural context (in order to remain untainted by the world), or they sidestep any issues that will jeopardize their popularity with their core constituency (in order to preserve unity in the church). Neither path is best. In the first case, leaders who disavow the idea of understanding and engaging the culture may think they've avoided cultural assimilation. In reality they and their followers remain blind to the ways they've been formed *unknowingly* by their cultural context.[3] In the second case, leaders who sidestep volatile issues compromise the breadth of the gospel's challenge to the culture by narrowing the scope of Scripture.

Multi-directional leaders approach the matter differently, recognizing that a global faith transcending all cultures will find points of affirmation and points of disassociation in every society. They are alert to the danger of cultural captivity, even among church leaders who brush off cultural concerns.

Christianity." Wells, quoted by Linda O. McMurry, *To Keep the Waters Troubled: The Life of Ida B. Wells* (Oxford: Oxford University Press, 2000), 74.

3.   "If we never deliberately think through ways to rightly contextualize gospel ministry to a new culture, we will unconsciously be deeply contextualized to some other culture." Timothy Keller, *Center Church: Doing Balanced, Gospel-Centered Ministry in Your City* (Grand Rapids, MI: Zondervan, 2012), 97.

Multi-directional leadership involves faithful versatility—the ability to see and respond to various challenges no matter how or where they arise. In order to gain a better glimpse of this leadership quality, let's consider two other spheres of life in which this kind of dexterity matters: business and parenting.

MULTI-DIRECTIONAL LEADERSHIP IN BUSINESS

We could look at several areas in which multi-directional leadership matters for savvy decision-making, but we'll stick with just one: how should an organization respond to an economic downturn or to a business initiative that failed to deliver anticipated revenue?

Leaders with *expertise in finance* will often urge the organization to cut expenses and manage to the bottom line until the situation stabilizes. Leaders with an *entrepreneurial spirit* will insist on investing in new initiatives that may lead to future growth. The ultimate decision-makers can't afford to be one-directional in this matter. Both paths, taken to the extreme, open organizations to significant business threats. The danger on one side is to manage expenses so tightly that opportunities for growth and investment are squashed. The danger on the other side is to invest in new initiatives without clear goals or discipline in spending. In both cases, the result could be further decline or, worse, financial disaster. A multi-directional leader will chart the more difficult course of finding ways to cut expenses *and* invest in the future.

MULTI-DIRECTIONAL LEADERSHIP IN PARENTING

Faithful versatility is required for parenting as well. A good mother will recognize when her child is most vulnerable to sin and temptation. Some kids wrestle with stubbornness and pride; others are overly compliant and lack self-confidence. An observant mother will be attuned to her children's weaknesses in order to care for them well.

The same is true when we give our children biblical instruction. I've come to cherish bedtime conversations when my kids bring up questions about Scripture and theology (although at times I've wondered if their goal is to delay "lights out"). Our 12-year-old daughter recently asked about God's purpose behind the pandemic that has up-ended all our plans, taken hundreds of thousands of lives, and left our country's economy weakened. Believing the virus to be a sign of divine judgment, she wondered why God caused so many people to lose their lives or livelihoods. In response, I took her to the book of Job and the story in John 9 of the man born blind, in order to guide her away from a simple correlation between particular suffering and specific sins. We don't understand all the ways of God, I told her, emphasizing what the Bible says about the mystery of God's sovereignty.

In an earlier conversation, our 16-year-old son commented on how we can't know what God is up to in this crisis or give any solid reason behind the trial. In response, I cited a number of biblical passages that stress God's sovereignty over earthly calamities and the opportunities for repentance and renewal that accompany every tragedy. I also mentioned the testimony of many Christians throughout history who had no trouble seeing God as active in human affairs, even in times of plague and other terrible circumstances.

Had someone listened to both of these conversations, they might have thought I was contradicting myself. In truth, I aimed to balance out my kids' perspectives by bringing to light other important biblical truths: an emphasis on mystery for my daughter who spoke of the pandemic in simple terms, and an emphasis on God's sovereign involvement for my son who seemed too agnostic about God's intention. Delivering biblical instruction to our children is an important aspect of parenting; being multi-directional involves a commitment to the glorious tensions and beautiful paradoxes we see in Scripture.

———

Whether we lead in business or in ministry, as parents or as pastors, the skill of multi-directional leadership remains vital. One-directional leaders leave the flock vulnerable and defenseless against threats from a different side of the field. Multi-directional leaders, though, spot various threats from different angles and adjust their leadership accordingly. We'll now explore some areas in which many church leaders struggle to lead in this way, and we'll look at some examples of multi-directional leadership in practice.

2

MULTI-DIRECTIONAL LEADERSHIP IN THEOLOGY AND PRACTICE

The landscape of evangelicalism appears increasingly fractured and polarized, especially in regard to political and theological debates. Leaders on the right are more attuned to the problems of progressivism and liberalism, while leaders on the left are more alert to the dangers of fundamentalism and isolationism. These fissures show up in various disputes (we will address a couple of these in a subsequent chapter), and we can see the fruit of this conflict in Christian institutions, in online discourse, and in local congregations.

In a fractured environment, pastors and other church leaders will tend to be drawn magnetically to one of the poles. Or, to return to our shepherding analogy, you are likely to feel most confident and effective in conflict when you gravitate to the side of the field where you've seen dangers and threats arise before. To change the picture again, imagine a soldier on a medieval battlefield, trained in wielding a sword in only one direction, whose armor is only on the front, without the intuition to turn around and gain a fuller sense of the battle at hand, and without protection in case he's attacked from behind.

The result? We grow strong in fighting off dangers from only one direction while remaining vulnerable to dangers that threaten the church from elsewhere. Church leaders afraid of slipping into an unbiblical quietism or theological fundamentalism ("just preach the gospel" without a corresponding emphasis on the gospel's implications for society) will remain alert to anything that could be a slippery slope to the right. But what if, in their revulsion to quietist fundamentalism, they stumble backward with no awareness of the pitfalls and traps associated with secular theories of justice and the social gospel?[1] Meanwhile, leaders fearful of the social gospel or other aspects of theological liberalism are ever alert to voices, partnerships, and statements that might indicate a slippery slope toward abandoning sound doctrine. But what if, in their rightful concern for theological fidelity, they stumble backward into pitfalls and traps associated with ethnic nationalism or other ideologies that would mute the Lord's commands and compromise the church's witness in society?

We need pastors and church leaders to sharpen their skills in fighting threats to the church that come from multiple directions. Unfortunately, many church members have come to prefer leaders who will point out the dangers coming from only one direction—while never offering a warning or uncovering the blind spots that may originate closer to home.

———

To be clear, no congregation and no church leader can succeed at being all things to all people, as if there is a perfect way to be multi-directional. Pastors shouldn't labor under the pressure to stay equally attuned to every danger. Every church brings together a unique blend of believers with various gifts and passions.

Collin Hansen makes this point in his book *Blind Spots*. Hansen celebrates the distinctive contributions made by different churches

---

1. By "social gospel," I mean the movement influenced by Walter Rauschenbusch, whose *Christianity and the Social Crisis* (1907) and *A Theology for the Social Gospel* (1917) eventually "saw Jesus as an important teacher [but] stripped the continuing reality from Christ. It made an ontological role for the Son of God unnecessary." Joseph Bottum, *An Anxious Age: The Post-Protestant Ethic and the Spirit of America* (New York: Image Books, 2014), 68.

and leaders, which he divides into three broad groupings: the courageous, the compassionate, and the commissioned.

- The courage group stands valiantly for the truth; it believes the problem today is "a failure of courage to walk the time-worn paths."[2]
- The compassion people stress service, listening, and engagement, especially for those hurt by the church or in their life experience.
- The "commissioned folks are all about building up the church and reaching the lost," full of "resolve to fulfill the Great Commission through creative new methods."[3]

Jesus works through churches that belong to all three of these groups, and we can celebrate the distinctive emphases we find in each. To fail to appreciate these distinctive gifts, as Tim Keller notes in his foreword, leaves us vulnerable, as "each group goes bad to the degree it distances itself from the others."[4] For example, a pastor who belongs to the courage group might celebrate his congregation's commitment to biblical fidelity, but if he is a one-directional leader, he may remain curiously unbothered by the church's lack of concern for the less fortunate and disadvantaged in the community, or their lack of passion for outreach that would fulfill the Great Commission. The pastor becomes blind to dangers from other sides of the field.

"The problem with blind spots," Hansen writes, "is that they tend to hide behind good traits. Your weakness is often the flip side of your strength."[5] Hansen and Keller imply that the way to lead faithfully in a polarized time is by listening to other groups, churches, and leaders who can alert you to dangers in your blind spot. The health of Christian churches across the country depends on the ability and willingness of leaders to respect people from groups that share the same unity

---

2. Collin Hansen, *Blind Spots: Becoming a Courageous, Compassionate, and Commissioned Church* (Wheaton, IL: Crossway, 2015), 32.

3. Hansen, *Blind Spots*, 33.

4. Tim Keller, foreword to Hansen, *Blind Spots*, 11.

5. Hansen, *Blind Spots*, 36.

in the gospel and commitment to the Bible, but whose outlook and emphasis differ in some respects.[6]

To extend the shepherding analogy, imagine several flocks gathered on a single field. Some flocks are off to one side, while other sheep remain close to another. Different shepherds, based on the location of their flocks, are naturally equipped to issue different warnings about dangers they see on their side. No shepherd can be perfectly multi-directional—always aware of every challenge from every direction—which is why it is important for the shepherds to communicate, to rely on each other in order to be faithful. This is also a reason for having a plurality of leaders with different emphases in the same congregation. The more pastors and church leaders rely on each other—united by doctrinal commitments yet attuned to different dangers—the more the church benefits from a multi-directional leadership culture.

Even in the New Testament, different writers display different emphases—all under the inspiration and guidance of the Holy Spirit. Consider the various shades and strokes given to us by the Gospel writers as they offer four different portraits of Jesus. Or watch how Paul spars with the Judaizers who threaten the precious doctrine of justification by faith alone (Gal. 1–3), while James fights off those who claim saving faith doesn't lead to good works (James 2:14–26). Were Paul and James opposed? No. They were two early church leaders, standing back-to-back, swords drawn, fighting off opposing enemies. The Spirit inspired them both.

The one-directional leader, by contrast, doesn't stand back-to-back with anyone. He fights alone. He seems unaware of dangers from other sides of the field and unconcerned that his skill in fighting off one or two big threats might leave him vulnerable to others. (Worse, he might train his sword on church leaders with different emphases.)

---

6. "What the Bible tells the church to do—witness, serve the needy, preach the Word, disciple people, worship—is so rich and multifaceted that no church will ever do all of them equally well, simply because no single church has all the spiritual gifts in equal proportions. While no church should stop trying to do everything that God calls it to do, no one church will fulfill these roles perfectly. So the city as a whole needs all kinds of churches. Recognizing the reality of multiple church models humbles us—we see we can't be all things to all people—and also encourages us to reach out and cooperate with other churches." Timothy Keller, *Serving a Movement: Doing Balanced, Gospel-Centered Ministry in Your City* (Grand Rapids, MI: Zondervan, 2016), 237.

One-directional leadership is common for a number of reasons, as we will see in a future chapter. Sometimes it's due to a leader's lack of historical awareness, minimal engagement with Christians in other cultures and countries, or simply enjoyment of the benefits of issuing one-sided warnings so as not to lose popularity or hear criticism from the people whose opinions matter most.

Multi-directional leaders not only recognize the reality of dangers from multiple angles, but also their need for different people to help their ministry and provide appropriate cautions. They know they have blind spots, and so they rely on others to help them see.

Multi-directional leadership shows up in Scripture and in the lives of leaders throughout church history. We'll look briefly at the biblical precedent for this faithful versatility before examining this manner of leadership as exemplified in an evangelical leader from the latter half of the 20th century.

PROVERBS

Multi-directional leadership shows up in proverbs that on the surface appear to be contradictory. "Don't answer a fool according to his foolishness or you'll be like him yourself," we're told in Proverbs 26:4. Yet in the next verse we read: "Answer a fool according to his foolishness or he'll become wise in his own eyes." This example is perhaps the starkest juxtaposition of two apparently contradictory statements in the Old Testament.

What is the point of this combination? The author demonstrates how wisdom requires dexterity, depending on the circumstance. There is danger in becoming the fool as you do battle with his foolishness. Likewise, there is danger in letting a fool run amok without correction.[7] Both dangers are real, and holding these inspired proverbs

---

7. Duane A. Garrett, *Proverbs, Ecclesiastes, Song of Songs*, New American Commentary 14 (Nashville, TN: B&H Publishing Group, 1993), 212.

together requires us to be attentive to the particulars of the situation before us.

JESUS'S LIFE

Jesus confounded the political and religious groups of his day. At times, he sounded like a superlative Pharisee, ramping up the application of the law. His vociferous condemnations of the Pharisees' hypocrisy made up some of the most notable aspects of his teaching ministry. But Jesus's intensification of the law was combined with surprising and overwhelming grace. He was radically inclusive in who he brought to his table of repentance, and yet he was radically exclusive in claiming it was only at his table that salvation could be found.

On one occasion, Jesus excoriated the Pharisees for dishonoring their parents by using the temple offering as an excuse for failing to care for their families (Mark 7:1–15). But the same Jesus disapproved of a man who wanted to bury his father before following him (Luke 9:59–62). And did he not later say that to follow him one must hate father, mother, sister, and brother (Luke 14:25–27)? Yet on the cross, one of his last words was in honor of his mother, as he entrusted her to the beloved disciple's care (John 19:25–27).

Was Jesus contradicting himself? No. He was responding to different idolatrous dangers. On one side, he opposed hypocritical attempts to slither out of obeying God's clear command to honor one's parents—a command he obeyed even as he died. On the other side, he communicated the danger of allowing one's family relationships to vie with himself for first place in the heart. Jesus deserves greater allegiance than anyone else, even one's closest loved ones. He resisted different dangers.

In the Sermon on the Mount, Jesus told his disciples to let their light shine, so that others may see their good works and give glory to God (Matt. 5:14–16). Moments later, we find Jesus instructing his disciples to do their good works (praying, fasting, and giving) without fanfare, so that the Lord will reward what's been done in secret (6:1–18). Which is it—good works in public or in secret? In the first instance, Jesus rules out the quietist temptation that would fail to show the love of God in deeds. In the second, he rules out the showy faith that cares more about self-glory than God's glory.

Jesus is consistent. His versatility isn't weakness, but strength. He recognizes different threats to his supremacy as King, and he addresses them accordingly. This is multi-directional leadership.

PAUL'S MINISTRY

We see the apostle Paul forfeit his rights for the sake of the kingdom and the advance of the gospel (1 Cor. 9). We also see him leverage his rights in order to appeal to the king (Acts 25). In one situation, Paul said circumcision was nothing and refused to have Titus circumcised (Gal. 2:1–5), while in another he was fine with Timothy being circumcised for missionary purposes because the gospel wasn't at stake (Acts 16:3).

In Paul's letters, the vices he wants Christians to avoid don't fit neatly into any category. We find everything from engaging in orgies to disobeying one's parents (e.g., Rom. 1:29–31; Col. 3:5–8; 1 Tim. 1:9–10; 2 Tim. 3:2–5; Titus 3:3). It's easy for us to screen out some of these sins as not being as serious as others, but Paul had no problem lumping them all together as "works of the flesh." As he encouraged the beloved community to embody the love and grace of Christ, he spoke to various problems that plague the flock of God. He didn't narrow his warnings to only certain kinds of sins.

JOHN STOTT'S EXAMPLE

Throughout this book, I'll point out different people who've modeled multi-directional leadership. We could reach back into church history for examples, such as Augustine making a profound case for free will in his battle against the Manicheans, and then leaning heavily on God's sovereignty and divine initiative in his debates with Pelagius. But a more recent example is the ministry of John Stott, one of the most prominent evangelicals of the latter 20th century, a leader alert to problems that could plague the church from multiple directions.

In the 1950s, standing against liberals in the Church of England who were scorning "fundamentalism," Stott defended the core tenets of the Christian faith, claiming the reasonableness of a Christianity that depends on divine revelation. He opposed the rationalists of his day who thought Christian dogma results in "stifling the mind."

In the same decade, Stott distanced himself from anti-intellectual fundamentalism that stood for "the bigoted rejection of all biblical criticism, a mechanical view of inspiration and an excessively literalistic interpretation of Scripture."[8] Stott, along with Billy Graham, Harold Ockenga, Carl Henry, and other leaders in the 1950s and '60s, gave shape to the neo-evangelical movement that sought to avoid the pitfalls of both separatist fundamentalism and compromised liberalism.

In the 1960s and '70s, Stott showed Christians the importance of critical thinking—arguments that became the classic *Your Mind Matters*.[9] He was concerned that evangelical Christians had succumbed to an anti-intellectual spirit. But in the same work, he observed the danger of an arid "hyper-intellectualism" that removes emotion and affection from the Christian life and turns the faith into a series of doctrinal affirmations without warmhearted love for God and neighbor. "God never intends knowledge to be an end in itself but always to be a means to some other end," he wrote.[10]

Here we see multi-directional leadership at work. Over against a liberal Christianity that gave priority to human reason—setting up the mind as the judge of divine revelation—Stott demoted human rationality by showing how it's affected by the fall. Over against anti-intellectual Christianity—whether in the guise of a superficial, emotion-based relationship with God or in the excesses of fundamentalist obscurantism—Stott argued for pursuing and developing a Christian mind as a vital aspect of discipleship.[11]

We can multiply the examples. When addressing the doctrine of Scripture, Stott warned against overemphasizing human authorship of the text to the exclusion of its divine authority. He also warned against subsuming the human personality of the authors to a divine-dictation theory.[12] In warning against worldliness, Stott called for "vigorous

---

8.   Tim Chester, *Stott on the Christian Life: Between Two Worlds* (Wheaton, IL: Crossway, 2020), 37–39.

9.   John Stott, *Your Mind Matters: The Place of the Mind in the Christian Life* (orig., 1972; Downers Grove, IL: InterVarsity Press, 2006).

10. Stott, *Your Mind Matters*, 79.

11. Chester, *Stott on the Christian Life*, 39–52.

12. Chester, *Stott on the Christian Life*, 83–84.

nonconformity." At the same time, he recognized Christians could fall into obscurantism—a place of nonconformity that doesn't bring us into contact with the world we're called to win.[13] In other words, he pleaded with Christians to maintain our saltiness and to not hide our light, while at the same time warning us of the danger of staying "in the saltshaker," preserving a mythical purity while losing touch with the people around us we're called to serve.

Stott's influential book on preaching, *Between Two Worlds*, called for sensitivity to both the ancient world *and* the modern world.[14] Some preachers allow the current moment to determine what can and must be preached, while other preachers present only the truth of Scripture without carefully applying it to their contemporary setting. But both fidelity and contextualization are necessary, without sacrificing one for the other, according to Stott. "We need more fidelity to Scripture and more sensitivity to people," he wrote. "Not one without the other, but both."[15]

STOTT AND THE CHURCH'S MISSION

Perhaps no area of division proved as important an arena for multi-directional leadership in the life of Stott than his understanding of the church's mission. Stott wanted to avoid dangers from multiple directions: ignoring social ministry (a temptation he saw in conservative circles) or allowing social ministry to swallow the urgency for verbal proclamation of the gospel (a tendency he saw in centrist and liberationist circles). His *Christian Mission in the Modern World* sought to chart a course of biblical comprehensiveness that would reject false choices.[16] Even if, like me, you believe aspects of Stott's vision need critique and revision (and, irenic as he was, he invited feedback and

13. Chester, *Stott on the Christian Life*, 58.
14. John Stott, *Between Two Worlds: The Challenge of Preaching Today* (Grand Rapids, MI: Wm. B. Eerdmans, 1982).
15. John Stott, *The Contemporary Christian: Applying God's Word to Today's World* (Downers Grove, IL: InterVarsity Press, 1995), 253.
16. John Stott, *Christian Mission in the Modern World* (orig., 1975; Downers Grove, IL: InterVarsity Press, 2008).

disagreement), don't miss how Stott could anticipate the church veering off course in more than one direction.[17]

Consider his words and actions. In 1968, when invited to address the World Council of Churches, Stott chastised the council for a dangerous imbalance in stressing social ministry by excluding or at least diminishing verbal evangelism. "The Assembly seemed to be intent on redefining mission largely in terms of material and social needs, and of such issues as race, refugees, world development, oppression, hunger, and war," his biographer Timothy Dudley-Smith later wrote. "To John Stott, this seemed symptomatic of the failure of the Council to live under the authority of Scripture [even though] he readily agreed the social dimension was of critical importance."[18]

Here is how Stott addressed the council:

> The Assembly has given its earnest attention to the hunger, poverty, and injustices of the contemporary world. Rightly so. I have myself been moved by it. But I do not find a comparable concern or compassion for the spiritual hunger of men. . . . The church's first priority . . . remains the millions and millions . . . who (as Christ and his apostles tell us again and again) being without Christ are perishing. . . . The World Council of Churches professes to acknowledge Jesus Christ as Lord. Well, the Lord Jesus Christ sent his church to preach the good news and make disciples; I do not see this Assembly as a whole eager to obey his command. The Lord Jesus Christ wept over the impenitent city which had rejected him; I do not see this Assembly weeping any similar tears.[19]

---

17. The merits of Stott's proposal regarding the church's mission are still up for debate. That discussion has since shifted into more nuanced distinctions delineated by scholars like Christopher Wright and Jonathan Leeman. The crux of the debate over Stott's proposal informs some of the conflicts about the gospel and justice even today. See Jason Sexton, ed., *Four Views on the Church's Mission*, Counterpoints (Grand Rapids, MI: Zondervan Academic, 2017). For an even broader debate of the church's mission, see Craig Ott, ed., *The Mission of the Church: Five Views in Conversation* (Grand Rapids, MI: Baker Academic, 2016).

18. Timothy Dudley-Smith, *John Stott: A Global Ministry, the Later Years* (Downers Grove, IL: Inter-Varsity Press, 2001), 125, comma added.

19. John Stott, *Christian Mission in the Modern World*, 32, comma added.

If that wasn't provocative enough, Stott also wrote,

> I believe that Jesus Christ is saying to the World Council about their concern for social justice what he said to the Pharisees about their concern for ceremonial observances: "these you ought to have done, without neglecting the others."[20]

As you can see, Stott was not afraid to challenge those who watered down the mission into social work. But in the years that followed, Stott also faced head-on those who thought the Great Commission was exclusively about evangelism without sufficient attention given to the church's social ministry. This perspective countered that of many participants in the evangelical Lausanne Conference in 1974 and resulted in a sharp debate in a committee meeting in 1975—a moment when Stott confronted Billy Graham, before being locked in a room with Peter Wagner until they could reach a compromise.[21]

Stott's vision prevailed at Lausanne, and his friendship with Graham survived the ordeal. Yet even here, Stott was self-critical, writing at the end of the trip in his diary,

> I think I was too quick on the draw. Although I do not regret anything I said, or even the way I said it, for I think I kept my cool and remained courteous, yet I was too quick to cast myself in the role of defending Lausanne and its covenant and of acting as protagonist for the Third World. I much regret this now, and wish I could learn to listen longer before speaking.[22]

Again, my point isn't to promote the particulars of Stott's position on the church's mission, or to praise all of his actions in pushing his perspective. (I disagree with a couple of Stott's theological conclusions.) My aim is to lift him up as a leader who could foresee and respond to threats to the church's witness from different directions, and who had the humility to constantly place his words and actions under scrutiny.

---

20. Dudley-Smith, *John Stott: A Global Ministry, the Later Years*, 125, punctuation adjusted for style.
21. Alister Chapman, *Godly Ambition: John Stott and the Evangelical Movement* (New York: Oxford University Press, 2012), 143.
22. John Stott, quoted in Roger Steer, *Basic Christian: The Inside Story of John Stott* (Downers Grove, IL: InterVarsity Press, 2010), 167.

In one assembly, we see him push hard against a reductionist social gospel; in another assembly, we see him push hard against a reductionist fundamentalism. He was neither a conservative warrior trained to spot only the dangers of liberalism, nor a progressive proponent trained to fight only the follies of fundamentalism. His theological commitments alerted him to problems coming at the church from multiple sides.

DEXTERITY AND VERSATILITY

Some may wonder if being multi-directional means being moderate in some way, as if we believe it is a virtue to pursue moderation for its own sake. Moderates look to find the middle or believe a third way must exist between opposite views. They desire to avoid ditches on one side or the other and so look for something middle-of-the-road. This moderate mindset easily succumbs to snobbery: *Everyone to my right is crazy, and everyone to my left is awful.* We could call this the Goldilocks fallacy—the idea that the moderate alone knows how to find and serve the one bowl of porridge that is neither too hot nor too cold but just right.

Multi-directional leadership must be distinguished from moderation. It is not about finding a perfect balance of competing interests and beliefs. It is, instead, a manner of leadership grounded in the unshakable conviction that *all* the truth revealed in Scripture must be deployed for the good of God's people. And, for truth to have its greatest influence, a leader must constantly be aware of the cultural context.[23] It's not about finding the middle between extremes, but about holding fiercely to *both extremes,* insofar as we see them in Scripture.

We'll see how this works in more detail in the next chapter. But first, consider how, in an article on consistency in leadership, Winston Churchill described the importance of dexterity:

A statesman, in contact with the moving current of events and anxious to keep the ship on an even keel and steer a steady course, may lean all

23. This is one of the primary points I make in *Eschatological Discipleship: Leading Christians to Understand Their Historical and Cultural Context* (Nashville, TN: B&H Academic, 2018).

his weight now on one side and now on the other. His arguments in each case, when contrasted, can be shown to be not only very different in character, but contradictory in spirit and opposite in direction: yet his object will throughout have remained the same. His resolves, his wishes, his outlook may have been unchanged, his methods may be verbally irreconcilable. We cannot call this inconsistency. In fact it may be claimed to be the truest consistency. The only way a man can remain consistent amid changing circumstances is to change with them while preserving the same dominating purpose.[24]

On the surface, dexterity may baffle the observer. But a closer look shows this kind of versatility is the outworking of a deeper consistency—one that crosses artificial lines and wards off opposing dangers because of the leader's singular purpose. This is the need of the hour: leaders who lean their weight now to one side and then the other, emphasizing a particular theological truth during a particular season and then a different truth in another.

Christian leadership requires an imagination formed by Scripture as well as a deep understanding of the current cultural moment, so we know what to say and when, what to emphasize and how, and what challenges to face and where. We need leaders who know their Bible and their times well enough to see threats coming from more than one direction. In the next chapter, we'll look at ways we can develop this type of leadership, before turning attention to some of the cultural trends that make it difficult to accomplish.

24. Winston Churchill, "Consistency in Leadership," *The Rotarian*, January 1936, 10.

3

DEVELOPING A MULTI-DIRECTIONAL SENSIBILITY

Where does multi-directional leadership come from? How can pastors increase their understanding of dangers that approach the flock from multiple directions? How does a leader develop this approach to life and practice?

In this chapter, I offer several suggestions that will enable us to grow in this skill. In order to develop a multi-directional sensibility, we must be faithful to Scripture, especially when it upsets our frameworks and challenges our assumptions. We must pay attention to alarms sounded by people inside and outside our immediate circles. And we must seek to better understand our tendencies and temptations, as well as those of the people we lead.

1. DELIGHT IN SCRIPTURE, EVEN WHEN IT CHALLENGES OUR SYSTEMS AND ASSUMPTIONS.

In the previous chapter, we looked at John Stott as a recent example of multi-directional leadership. One of the greatest influences on Stott was Charles Simeon, a well-known pastor who lived from 1759 to 1836 and devoted 54 years of ministry to Cambridge University and Holy

Trinity Church.[1] Facing decades of public scorn and constant opposition, Simeon persevered. He gave pastoral guidance to the influential group of evangelicals known as the Clapham Sect, which included Hannah More and William Wilberforce, leaders largely responsible for bringing an end to slavery in England.[2]

We see Simeon's multi-directional leadership in action through his expository sermons and the instructions he gave to the young men he trained. "My endeavor is to bring out of Scripture what is there," Simeon wrote, "and not to thrust in what I think might be there. I have a great jealousy on this head; never to speak more or less than I believe to be the mind of the Spirit in the passage I am expounding."[3]

During his lifetime, debates between Calvinists and Arminians loomed large, but Simeon, though doctrinally more Calvinistic, expressed his desire to make "Bible Christians," not "system Christians." As Chris Armstrong remarks,

> He recognized in the Bible certain paradoxes and antinomies that simply could not—and must not—be reconciled. We can eliminate neither divine sovereignty nor human responsibility, he insisted, since the Bible teaches both. . . . For Simeon, "it is not *one* extreme we are to go to, but *both* extremes." . . . Simeon . . . acted as a barrier-crossing and bridge-building figure at a crucial moment in the church's history.[4]

This sensibility is key to understanding multi-directional leadership. "The truth is not in the middle," Simeon wrote, "and not in one

1.   For brief biographical sketches of Simeon, see chapter 7, "Charles Simeon: Overcoming Wounds and Shaping Leaders," in Chris Armstrong, *Patron Saints for Postmoderns: Ten from the Past Who Speak to Our Future* (Downers Grove, IL: InterVarsity Press, 2009); Randall J. Gruendyke, "Charles Simeon: Faithful Shepherd to Hostile Sheep," in *12 Faithful Men: Portraits of Courageous Endurance in Pastoral Ministry*, eds. Collin Hansen and Jeff Robinson (Grand Rapids, MI: Baker Books, 2018); "Charles Simeon" in John Piper, *21 Servants of Sovereign Joy: Faithful, Flawed, and Fruitful* (Wheaton, IL: Crossway, 2018), 298–325.
2.   William Wilberforce once said of him, "Simeon with us—his heart glowing with love of Christ. How full he is of love, and of desire to promote the spiritual benefit of others. Oh! That I might copy him as he Christ." Cited in Hugh Evans Hopkins, *Charles Simeon of Cambridge* (Eugene, OR: Wipf and Stock, 2012), 166.
3.   H. C. G. Moule, *Charles Simeon* (London: Methuen & Co., 1892), 97.
4.   Armstrong, *Patron Saints for Postmoderns: Ten from the Past Who Speak to Our Future*, 143. Emphasis in original.

extreme, but in both extremes."[5] For this reason, he can't be classified as middle-of-the-road. His choice to set Scripture above systems (even the one to which he held) wasn't motivated by personal comfort or the desire to never offend anyone. He willingly endured constant ridicule and social ostracism in a period of English history marked by hardheartedness toward the gospel. It would've been *easier* to be one-directional, to fall into the trap of cultivating just one segment of his community that would applaud his efforts and stances and yet remain safely ensconced from any serious critique from his pulpit. Instead, when he discovered texts that appeared to be in tension, Simeon asked, "Why . . . must these things be put in opposition to each other, so that every advocate for one of these points must of necessity controvert and explode the other?"[6]

Simeon recognized vital truths in Scripture and clung to them tenaciously, allowing truth's paradoxical power to have its full effect—no matter what categories might be crossed or who might be troubled. Complementary truths were like "the wheels in a clock mechanism, apparently moving in opposite directions yet working together to achieve a common end."[7] Tim Chester sums up the approach this way: "We do not have to worry about over-affirming something as long as we do not let go of its complementary truth. So we have two strong truths which we affirm with all our might."[8]

This approach resembles the apologetic insight of G. K. Chesterton, whose *Orthodoxy* makes a similar case for paradox—holding together truths that appear as if they're opposed.[9] The point isn't to find the balance or stay in the middle—to water down two apparently contradictory truths so they can mesh more easily. When faced with competing passions or doctrines, the goal isn't to seek "an amalgam or compromise," he wrote, "but both things at the top of their energy; love and wrath both burning." This collision of truths is the key to orthodox theology, such as the doctrine of the divinity and humanity

---

5. William Carus, ed., *Memoirs of the Life of the Rev. Charles Simeon* (New York: Robert Carter, 1847), 352.

6. Charles Simeon, *Horae Homileticae* (1832), 1:xvii. Cited in Chester, *Stott on the Christian Life*, 59.

7. Chester, *Stott on the Christian Life*, 59.

8. Chester, *Stott on the Christian Life*, 61.

9. G. K. Chesterton, *Orthodoxy* (New York: John Lane Company, 1908).

of Christ: "Christ was not a being apart from God and man, like an elf, nor yet a being half human and half not, like a centaur, but both things at once and both things thoroughly, very man and very God."[10]

For multi-directional leaders, faithfulness to Scripture isn't about avoiding extremes (such as believing Scripture is *either* divine revelation *or* the work of human authors), but *combining* extremes (the Bible is God's Word *through* and *to* humanity). We find delight in whatever the Bible teaches, not merely the truths one group prefers to emphasize or elevate. We seek to speak the truth in all its glory, recognizing that any attempt to overemphasize one truth to the exclusion of another, or to water down a truth in order to make it more palatable, will result in subtle distortions that subvert our witness.

Stott was right to warn leaders of this ever-present danger: "If the devil cannot induce us to deny Christ, he will get us to distort Christ instead. In consequence lopsided Christianity is widespread, in which we overemphasize one aspect of a truth, while underemphasizing another."[11] On a similar note, Collin Hansen points out how easy it is to distort our presentation of Christ by focusing primarily on what we love most about him:

> Almost everyone loves something about Jesus. Some of us love his courage to endure the scorn and shame of the cross. Others love his compassion to associate with sinners and liberate the oppressed. Still more love his commission for the disciples to heal the sick and cast out demonic spirits. It's harder, though, to love the real Jesus who does all this and more, then calls us to follow in his steps. We often seize on one aspect of his character and ministry and brandish it as a weapon against other believers. And we rope our partial Jesus into some of the nastiest conflicts.[12]

We mustn't settle for a lopsided Christianity or one-directional leadership that would present a distorted vision of Christ to the world. We're called to delight in all the truth of the Bible, and to love and represent Jesus as he is described there.

10. Chesterton, *Orthodoxy*, 169.
11. Stott, *The Contemporary Christian*, 375.
12. Hansen, *Blind Spots*, 103.

2. LISTEN CAREFULLY TO PEOPLE (INCLUDING YOUR CRITICS) WHO SOUND VARIOUS ALARMS.

One-directional leaders are adept at sounding alarms; it's just that their warnings are generally directed to one side of the field. The narrow scope of the books they read and voices they heed limits their ability to receive cautions and warnings—except for those they've already identified. The problem isn't that one-directional leaders are alarmist, but that they aren't alarmist *enough*. Like a radio tuned to only one frequency, they may perceive a particular threat clearly but remain deaf to other warning bells.

If we're to develop a multi-directional sensibility, we must recognize there is something valuable we can glean from one-directional leaders: their warnings are often right. Don't dismiss the skills of the one-directional leader in fighting off a threat coming from a particular side of the field. We must learn to recognize and receive whatever is true, even when the truth comes from unexpected directions and sources. And sometimes, to our surprise, it may be from otherwise unbalanced, one-directional leaders that we encounter vital truths.

Even multi-directional leaders will never be totally balanced or equally adept at fending off every threat. Our goal is to develop an awareness of threats arising from different sides of the field. That's why we'll need to rely on other shepherds for wisdom and warning. We grow more equipped in fighting off various dangers when we tune into more than one frequency.

When someone from a different side of the field sounds a warning, you have a choice: ignore the counsel, or give it careful consideration. The natural response, of course, is to reject counsel that comes as critique. When someone alerts you to a threat to the flock, initially you may feel slighted: *Does this person think I am blind for not emphasizing this danger?* You may be inclined to brush off the concern. The better response, though, is to listen carefully and discern if the concern is valid. If it is, then assess the size of the threat. One-directional leaders often overstate the immediate danger of a narrow set of concerns. But this overstatement doesn't mean there is no validity to the warning.

Stott often found creative solutions and, in a number of areas, steered a path for evangelicals because he listened carefully when

certain positions or postures provoked strong reactions from critics. When people were suddenly up in arms about a particular point
of doctrine or practice, Stott would ask, "Why did they feel this so
strongly?" Instead of instantly dismissing their concerns as invalid or
overstated, he sought to discern what these critics believed was in danger of being lost. "What is it that they want to safeguard?" he would
ask. "The extraordinary thing was that in many cases you find that
you want to safeguard it too. And then you reach the point of creative
development or creative solutions."[13]

This posture requires humility, a virtue that doesn't come naturally to anyone. We all need counsel, even from our fiercest critics.[14] For
this reason, pastors and church leaders who want to grow in their ability to recognize various dangers will deliberately seek voices from other groups, listen carefully to their critics, and read books from different perspectives—not so they will be seen as cultured or balanced, but
so they develop, over time, the ability to recognize multiple threats.

3. KNOW YOURSELF AND THE DANGERS TO WHICH YOU'RE SUSCEPTIBLE.

Multi-directional leadership requires honest and accurate self-assess-
ment. As a pastor or other church leader, you need to know yourself
and your tendencies. You need to recognize your weaknesses and
vulnerabilities. Like a teenager learning to drive, even if you can't see
your blind spot, you should at least know *where* the car you can't see is
most likely to be. You need to know which set of dangers you're prone
to miss.

Why is it important to know yourself and the direction you would
most likely drift toward error? Again, the goal isn't to arrive at a place
of perfect balance or moderation whereby you *decrease* your skill in
responding to dangers you've learned to spot; your aim is simply to
better guard the flock from threats you're not accustomed to fighting.

13.   John Stott, "Rehabilitating Discipleship: An Interview with John Stott," *Prism*, July–August
      1995, cited in Chester, *Stott on the Christian Life*, 174–75.
14.   "Bless your critics for their honesty. They do not criticize you to be a blessing to you, but the
      end product may be the same." Calvin Miller, *Preaching: The Art of Narrative Exposition* (Grand
      Rapids, MI: Baker Academic, 2010), 38.

If you've been lifting weights with one arm, so only those muscles have developed, the solution isn't to stop lifting altogether and thus lose your strength, but to lift with the other arm to bring both sides to a similar level.

In order to develop this multi-directional sensibility, you must assess yourself and learn to recognize where your mental muscles are underdeveloped. Examine your tendencies in order to discern your vulnerabilities. Ask yourself:

- If my ministry were to distort the gospel in some way, what kind of distortion would it likely be?
- If I were to drift theologically, in what direction would it happen?
- How might my temperament or personality affect my tendencies? Do I naturally gravitate toward controversy (and am perhaps prone to being pugnacious), or do I naturally want to avoid conflict (and am perhaps prone to being a coward)?
- Considering my strengths and weaknesses as a shepherd, where is the flock I lead most susceptible to danger?

These questions matter because they help us recognize how easily our revulsion toward one error can leave us vulnerable to another. Along these lines, C. S. Lewis writes,

> [The Devil] always sends errors into the world in pairs—pairs of opposites. And he always encourages us to spend a lot of time thinking which is the worst. You see why, of course? He relies on your extra dislike of one to draw you gradually into the opposite one. But do not let us be fooled. We have to keep our eyes on the goal and go straight through between both errors. We have no other concern than that with either of them.[15]

Errors don't always present themselves in the way Lewis describes; sometimes they come in more varied combinations (not just pairs). Still, his warning is apt. Your antipathy toward one set of errors might make a different set attractive. It's important to know yourself and

---

15.   C. S. Lewis, *Mere Christianity* (New York: Simon and Schuster, 1996), 161.

which way you lean, so you'll be extra vigilant toward dangers approaching from a different side.

As an example, let's return to John Stott and the debate among evangelicals about the church's mission. In some churches and denominations, when social action has been given a major role in the church's mission, the urgency of evangelism has disappeared and (eventually) the gospel has been swallowed up by social concern. Meanwhile, in other churches and denominations where the emphasis has focused narrowly on personal conversion, congregations have often been quietly complicit in social inaction.

Both cases present real dangers. In order to know yourself and the dangers to which you're most susceptible, you must move beyond merely *seeing* the different dangers and ask a more targeted question: *Which of these dangers do I feel more acutely?* By recognizing your visceral reaction to one of the threats, you're able to see more clearly the opposing threat that may deserve more of your attention. For example, if you're constantly on guard against anything that smacks of the "social gospel," you may need to ensure your congregation remains committed to obeying the second greatest commandment (Matt. 22:36–40). Is your congregation firm on the priority of evangelism but wobbly in spreading God's love through service to the world?

On the other hand, if you're on guard against any effort to privatize the gospel—to set up a wedge between individual conversion and addressing injustice in society—you may need to ensure your congregation remains committed to keeping the cross, not a cause (however righteous), as the center of focus. Is your congregation active in serving the community, but passive in spreading the gospel and urging people to repent of sin and trust in Jesus for salvation?

Knowing yourself also means taking a closer look at your experiences, in order to see how your intuitions and perceptions have been shaped by your past. For example, if you grew up in a church with authoritarian leaders, you may be inclined to set up guardrails that prohibit pastors from exercising power. On the other hand, if your church experience was marked by a free-for-all, in which pastors had little authority and members were never held accountable for sin, you may be inclined to stress the authority structures the New Testament prescribes for protecting the flock.

Both responses are understandable in light of one's experience. But the apostle Paul encourages the Thessalonians to "respect those who labor among you and are over you in the Lord and admonish you" (1 Thess. 5:12, ESV). His vision is for the shepherd to be both *among* and *over* the sheep. One danger emphasizes "over"—the shepherd begins to lord authority over others, in contradiction to Jesus's picture of servant leadership (Mark 10:41–45). The other danger emphasizes "among"—the shepherd is treated just like everyone else, and the congregation isn't led. In contrast to these dangers, we find a beautiful blend in Scripture for church leadership that takes place both *among* and *over* the congregation.

The multi-directional leader discerns any leanings or biases that spring from temperament or experience. Though your leanings may be understandable in light of your history, your past doesn't give you a pass on being faithful to God's Word. Know yourself, take stock of your history, and recognize why you lean the way you do. In the end, you must submit to Scripture and stay alert to the way your tendencies may lead you to downplay dangers from other sides.

4. KNOW YOUR PEOPLE AND THE DANGERS TO WHICH THEY ARE SUSCEPTIBLE.

In addition to knowing your own susceptibility to error, pastors and other church leaders must know their cultural context and the people they serve. In an era of constant communication, you may follow news, commentary, and debates happening in other parts of the country and around the world. Greater cultural awareness is good, but not if it comes at the expense of knowing the concerns and challenges facing the people entrusted to you. Multi-directional leaders not only know their own strengths and weaknesses, but also the tendencies and leanings of the flock. *How well do you know the sheep you lead? If the sheep were to wander, would it be in this direction or that? How would the sheep respond to different dangers that arise?*

While some Christian leaders have influence that extends beyond their particular context, the local church remains ground zero for pastoral influence. The pastor serves *a* church, not *all* churches. No one is a world pastor. God calls you to lead a particular people—to recognize their strengths and weaknesses and remain aware of the direction they would most likely wander.

Some leaders may notice a variety of impulses in their people. Different sensibilities often overlap in the same congregation. What if some sheep are more inclined to wander one way, while others would pull the flock in a different direction? In *The Screwtape Letters*, C. S. Lewis imagined how the demons might cancel the effects of church attendance by pushing Christians into factions within the congregation: "[I]f your patient can't be kept out of the church, he ought at least to be violently attached to some party within it," Screwtape writes.[16] "All extremes except extreme devotion to the Enemy are to be encouraged."[17]

In these cases, the faithful shepherd must exercise multi-directional leadership by preaching in ways that address more than one potential avenue for going astray and—through personal counseling and conversation—guiding church members along the road of faithfulness. As we saw before, church leaders are like physicians who prescribe different medicines for different maladies. As long as the different tendencies of people within the church don't threaten the unity of the body, the versatile pastor can use these sensibilities to the advantage of multi-directional leadership, so that these groups keep each other from drifting into error.

Still, even in churches that may have a number of factions, a congregation is often more likely to wander in one direction than another. Churches not in danger of splitting may still be in danger of drifting (see Heb. 2:1–4; Rev. 2:4). Multi-directional leaders will pay attention to the congregation in order to discern its direction and provide guidance.

Giving attention to the flock sounds basic, but it may be harder today than in the past, especially when Christian leaders can easily become more consumed with what is happening nationally than locally. On the one hand, focusing on national trends or developments in other parts of the world can help us avoid a tunnel vision that fails to note cultural currents that may soon affect the flock. On the other,

16.   C. S. Lewis, *The Screwtape Letters* (New York: HarperOne, 2001), 84.

17.   Lewis, *The Screwtape Letters*, 33.

when our primary focus becomes the global or national context, our vision for local church ministry can be distorted.

The reality is, in any church, you're likely to find multiple things are true at the same time, depending on the context. One-directional leaders often seize stories that prove the reality of dangers they see clearly—and wave away stories that challenge their preferred narrative. In this way, they feel affirmed in their one-directional warnings. Multi-directional leaders, by contrast, take heed of different stories from different churches—not to confirm their intuitions but to better understand how to minister in their local community. For example, some leaders warn about churches sliding into a new form of the social gospel, with secular ideologies related to racial injustice leading to a departure from the faith. Is this slide real for some churches? Yes. Meanwhile, other leaders warn about churches overlooking persistent racial prejudice among their members, and downplaying a Christian's responsibility to affirm the dignity and equality of all who are made in God's image. Is this a real problem in some churches? Yes. Who is right? Who is wrong?

Isn't it possible both are right? In a country as big as the United States, surely there are churches whose members are in danger of substituting the message of Jesus's cross and resurrection with political activism and community development. And surely there are churches whose members wink at racial prejudice and shrug at evidence of racial injustice. Both problems can exist in different churches *at the same time*. The multi-directional leader may be aware of various threats to churches across the country, but the question that looms largest is this: *What is true of the church I am called to lead? Which threats do we face? What dangers are on our horizon?* Again, the leader's primary focus must be local, not national.

Paying attention to the people closest to you is challenging in a media environment that tempts us to paint in broad strokes and fixate on omnipresent problems. As a result, "we tend to confuse what is most depicted with what is what most real," Samuel James observes. "Our concern is disproportionately directed toward things that loom large in the media hive, because that's where our awareness of The World comes from." In this environment, the one-directional leader is likely to "express the public implications of our faith in the direction of people least likely to heed our message, and on current events least likely to be urgent in actual churches."[18]

As a pastor, you may be inclined to rail against the push for polyamorous relationships you just read about in *The New York Times*. But what if the more pressing problem for people in your congregation is pornography, cohabitation, or the understanding of marriage as capstone to life and means of self-expression rather than cornerstone for the future and means to sanctification?[19] Or perhaps you belong to a church that has stressed marriage in ways disproportionate to biblical teaching, leaving little room for championing the call to singleness and welcoming as a church family those who are unmarried.[20]

As James explains, "My point is that two things can be true at the same time, but in different places and because of different things. . . . We fail to see this only because we look with one eye closed."[21] Multi-directional leaders work hard to keep both eyes open: be aware of wider cultural trends, but be most attentive to the pressing needs of your particular congregation.

These four suggestions will help us develop the kind of dexterity and versatility required for multi-directional leadership. In order to implement these instructions, however, we need to overcome cultural forces that conspire to prevent this kind of development. In the next chapter, we'll look at these obstacles and barriers.

18. Samuel James, "Which Enemy? Which Doorstep?," Letter and Liturgy, https://letterandliturgy.wordpress.com/2020/08/21/which-enemy-which-doorstep.

19. For an explanation of how expressive individualism has influenced our society's understanding of marriage, see Timothy and Kathy Keller, *On Marriage* (New York: Penguin Books, 2020), 1–41. Similar assumptions are true of believers across the world, not only in the West. See Mark Regnerus, *The Future of Christian Marriage* (New York: Oxford University Press, 2020).

20. See Sam Allberry, *7 Myths about Singleness* (Wheaton, IL: Crossway, 2019).

21. James, "Which Enemy? Which Doorstep?"

4

OBSTACLES TO MULTI-DIRECTIONAL LEADERSHIP

Many factors today conspire against the formation of multi-directional leaders: tribalism, institutional loyalties, online habits, and the desire to stay safely ensconced in a community that only guards against dangers we already foresee. These forces are at work in evangelical circles, where we often reward voices that cater to our sensibilities and then lift up as prophets anyone who can score points for our side. When we succumb to these tendencies, we close our eyes and ears to the multifaceted dangers lurking in the shadows behind us, and we leave the Bride of Christ vulnerable to other manifestations of the spirit of the age.

In this chapter, we'll look at several of these obstacles that stand in the way of multi-directional leadership—challenges that pull us back toward being one-directional. Preparing for these challenges and recognizing these barriers will aid us in our pursuit of faithful versatility.

1. WE FEAR THE BAD TRAJECTORY.

The first barrier to multi-directional leadership is an often-unstated fear of the bad trajectory. Perhaps the pastor wants to avoid the fate of other leaders who, once they started down a road, eventually adopted positions no longer in line with biblical teaching. Made aware of the path leading to dangers on one side of the field, the leader stakes out positions and builds fences in order to protect the flock from any movement in that direction. One-directional leaders fear the bad trajectory—the slippery slope to theological or moral disaster.

We shouldn't dismiss this impulse. Noticing a trajectory is an aspect of growing in wisdom. Some slopes really are slippery. Of course, we should never accuse people of holding positions they don't. Neither should we insist that a certain viewpoint always leads to problems. But wisdom would have us recognize that ideas have consequences. It can be appropriate to warn others about a trajectory of thought or action that might lead away from the truth. The problem with one-directional leaders isn't their concern regarding the slippery slope or the bad trajectory; it's that they forget how trajectories can go in more than one direction. Worried about the slippery slope on one side, they miss the slope on the other.

Consider the historical example of hyper-Calvinism. In an effort to preserve the distinctives of Reformed soteriology—to avoid a slippery slope toward Arminian views—some pastors in previous generations concluded that "saving faith in Christ cannot be the duty of sinners, for if we exhort the dead in trespasses and sins to trust in Christ we are attributing a power to them which they do not have."[1] Therefore, they opposed calling sinners to repentance. They blasted William Carey for his missionary passion and Charles Spurgeon for his evangelistic pleas. Hyper-Calvinism developed when certain teachers, on guard against doctrinal drift that would diminish God's sovereignty, failed to see how far *they* were drifting from the biblical teaching regarding human responsibility. In avoiding one bad trajectory, they followed another.

Ironically, the fear of the bad trajectory can backfire in a surprising way. By missing the opportunity to train people to see multifaceted dangers, leaders can make the congregation more vulnerable to the very threats they were most worried about. When challenges come from an unexpected direction, and when the sheep are shocked to find the shepherd unaware of a threat from that side at all, it's easy to lose

---

1.   Iain Murray, *Spurgeon v. Hyper-Calvinism: The Battle for Gospel Preaching* (London: Banner of Truth, 1995), 58.

faith in the shepherd and gravitate toward the other side of the field. The danger most feared by the shepherd can become the direction for the flock.

Multi-directional leadership requires us to overcome the obstacle of fearing a bad trajectory. Faith, not fear, should characterize our posture as we engage in theology and practice. In sum, we should be alert not just to a bad trajectory from one side, but to troubling trajectories (plural) that can lead us astray in a number of ways.

2. WE RISK LOSING STATUS.

Another obstacle is that multi-directional leadership requires us to take a risk. When we decide to warn the flock of dangers from multiple directions, we risk losing status.

One-directional leaders worry that if they point out a troubling trajectory in the opposite direction, they may open themselves to the charge they're no longer sound or solid regarding the dangers they usually point out. In order to maintain their reputation, then, they let dangers they can see out of the corner of their eye encroach upon the flock because they don't want to lose face.

This is a constant temptation for church leaders. A biblical understanding of sin explains why we long for affirmation and justification; often our hearts are more concerned with *looking* right than *being* right. We want the approval of others, so we avoid warnings that might endanger that affirmation. In a word, we're quicker to protect our reputation than our flocks. What's more, in order to combat the uneasy sense that we've settled for one-directional leadership, we succumb to confirmation bias, in which we seek out new evidence to back our one-directional warnings.

It would be easy, for example, for a pastor or church leader with experience in a more traditional church to do away with certain cultural trappings that feel old-school, in order to create the vibe of "We're not your grandmother's church." The type of people attracted to that church may, however, also assume that the church has done away with traditional Christian doctrines and practices, and church leaders may turn quiet on contested matters of doctrine to avoid losing status or the support of those they've reached with the new church model.

Once again, the temptation is to do whatever it takes to hold on to others' approval.

Multi-directional leadership requires us to reject the fear of losing status. We must pursue faithful versatility no matter the risks, and never sacrifice our convictions in order to satisfy followers or peers.

3. WE WILL BE MISUNDERSTOOD ONLINE.

Another barrier to multi-directional leadership is the nature of online communication today. The environment created by social media and the widespread availability of online resources may hinder leaders from demonstrating multi-directional skills when addressing specific audiences.

In the past, when a ministry leader was invited to address a group of people, the leader would tailor the message for *that* group in *that* context. The content of the message would focus on the strengths and weaknesses of the audience, and the speaker's commendation or warning would be limited to the people present. (That's why, in the pre-internet age, John Stott could sound like a fiery fundamentalist when addressing the World Council of Churches and like a social-ministry champion when addressing Lausanne. He knew his audience, and he tailored his remarks to the dangers he perceived in *that* group.)

The world is different today. Because of the accessibility of conference talks and the livestreaming of panel discussions and the rapid spread of social media reports even when there is no broadcast, anything a leader says can be taken from one context and planted in another, leading to bizarre assumptions and conclusions.

Picture a leader at a conference devoted to the amazing grace of God in the gospel. Imagine the leader issues a warning about "cheap grace" that fails to stress the sanctifying work of the Spirit, concerned that many of the conference participants may be drawn toward antinomianism. A qualified, targeted warning to this leader's tribe could be taken out of context online and used as evidence by people who want to force a strong disjunction between preaching grace and pursuing holiness. Imagine now the same scenario on the other side. A leader known for stressing the lordship of Christ, and pointing out the dangers of using grace as an excuse for laxity in pursuing holiness, stands before an audience of like-minded individuals and warns about legalism or the subtle ways in which a Christian might revert to a law-centered life. In both cases, the leader will likely be forced to issue clarifications and explain the nature of the original warning, in order to keep unfair perceptions from hardening online amid a social-media storm.

These examples apply to ministry leaders whose influence extends beyond the local congregation. But the same can be true of any pastor. A sermon podcast directed toward a specific need in a congregation can be taken out of context by someone online who may assume the pastor's focus on a particular need implies disregard for a different need. The nature of online communication and the widespread availability of resources make it easier than ever for a multi-directional leader's warnings to be misconstrued.

Multi-directional leaders know how easily they may be misunderstood or their words manipulated. We must be attentive to ways our statements could be taken out of context and promoted online by people suspicious of our motives. But that must not stop us from speaking the right word at the right time to the right people.

4. OUR WARNINGS MAY BE USED TO DISCREDIT US.

This challenge flows from doing ministry in a world of constant connectivity. Since everything that gets said (regardless of intended audience) has the potential of being overheard online, anything we say can be stripped of context and spread on various social-media platforms or in personal conversation.

What happens next? As soon as a leader demonstrates the ability and desire to fight off threats from multiple directions, some of the people who were once sympathetic to the leader's perspective feel betrayed, and they seize statements and marshal evidence to show that the leader must've moved to the opposing side. The one who warns about a threat to the right must be a closet liberal. Or the one who warns about a threat to the left must be a fundamentalist.

Preferring to follow leaders who only oppose threats coming from one direction, some Christians see multi-directional warnings as evidence of doctrinal drift and then begin to discredit whatever the leader says. The moment a leader's words challenge them, they quick-ly write off the leader, even if they've benefited from that ministry in the past. They'd rather destroy the leader's credibility than receive further counsel.

The rush to discredit leaders leaves us all impoverished. It breeds an overly suspicious attitude that makes it harder to receive legitimate warnings. As a result, the kind of leader we need to hear the most is the very leader to whom our ears are closed.

Multi-directional leaders must recognize the risks in issuing warn-ings that may upset their followers. We should do whatever we can to avoid unnecessary obstacles or easy misunderstandings in our com-munication. Still, we can't allow our warnings to be worded so vaguely or generally as to lose their potency. We must be courageous in alert-ing people to multiple dangers, even if we know our warnings could be misused to discredit us.

5. TRIBALISM AND POLARIZATION ENCOURAGE ONE-DIRECTIONAL WARNINGS.

The battle to overcome this obstacle happens in the heart. In order to avoid being misunderstood or discredited, leaders soon find it easier to say whatever they're expected to say. In other words, if you're known for fighting threats from one direction only (and if you're celebrated for your skill in the fight), then the temptation is strong to stay in your lane, keep issuing one-directional warnings, and avoid speaking to spe-cific pitfalls most likely to trip up your followers.

The reason so many people have little patience for warnings about dangers coming from multiple directions is that much of our society has slipped into an all-or-nothing battle, in which legitimizing the concerns of people outside our tribe appears suspect. Certain people are more united by disdain for their opponents than by something they affirm. In evangelical circles, many of our online squabbles appear to be driven by similar sentiments. That's why it's acceptable to cast doubt or aspersion on anyone in another camp within evangelicalism, but unacceptable for a leader in one camp to say about another, "I think they make a good point; we should consider this critique." Such admission betrays the cause.

No wonder we prefer one-directional leadership. It's easier. It's simpler. It's clear-cut. You convince yourself that you're faithful in fighting the dangers you see before you, without the slightest concern about backing up into dangers behind you.

Multi-directional leaders must have the courage to pursue godly leadership according to the qualifications we see in the New Testament, and wisdom requires us to recognize and reject the rules of polarization we've inherited. If the truth transcends our tribal loyalties, and if dangers do appear from multiple directions, then we can't allow polarization to become an excuse for silence. When you accept these new constraints, adopt worldly categories, and seek the applause of those who agree with your assessment of threats from one direction, the power of polarization increases. To slip into such worldliness will make it even harder for the next generation of leaders to emerge with the skills and courage necessary to fend off threats from multiple directions.

6. OUR WOUNDS TEMPT US TO SWITCH SIDES.

There's another barrier to multi-directional leadership. It's whenever a pastor or church leader moves from being one-directional to multi-directional, and then becomes one-directional again—only this time they're going in the other direction.

The shepherd takes a long look around the field and sees wolves encroaching from an unexpected direction. The leader recognizes the dangers of one-directional leadership and decides to issue multi-directional warnings. As we saw earlier, in a polarized era multi-directional warnings will prompt some to question your theological direction and overall soundness. *Do the multi-directional warnings indicate theological slippage? Is the leader now open to theological aberration? Has the leader lost sight of established dangers?* In this way, the warnings of the multi-directional leader—instead of indicating a desire to protect the flock from multifaceted dangers—accumulate as evidence that the shepherd has strayed.

Ironically, this line of attack and process of discrediting, which in the beginning may be totally unjustified, can lead to its fulfillment. Such criticism can actually make multi-directional leaders *more* vulnerable to straying than they might've been before. Here's how the scenario works out.

When you take arrows from those once friendly toward you, you feel the wounds deeply. In response to the pain you've felt for stepping out of line, you gravitate toward other pastors and leaders who've been in similar circumstances and experienced similar hurts. But instead of receiving counsel from those who've faced the sting of rejection and betrayal and yet share your convictions, you commiserate with people who belong to other theological or political tribes. When this happens, wounded shepherds often encourage the worst impulses in each other. Self-pity, a subtle form of pride, takes root. Your wounds get nursed, not healed, in a context of friendship built on commiseration instead of commitment to the truth.

Here's the great peril for multi-directional leaders: commiseration overcomes conviction. The people with whom you feel a sense of camaraderie in your hurt and pain may be the ones to lead you, ironically, back to one-directional leadership. Except this time, the direction of your warnings is the opposite from your warnings before. Your old theological opponents become your new emotional allies. Now, for example, the stalwart conservative who once issued warnings about theological drift to the left only sounds the alarm about problems to the right. Alert to threats you used to ignore, you issue warnings in a new direction but stop addressing the dangers you used to rightly warn about. Over time, you develop a new set of followers animated by your new brand of one-directional leadership. And eventually, the fears that drive one-directional leadership now work in the opposite way, leading you to abandon previous convictions. What's more, you become a mascot for the other side because you switched teams. So the incentives to revert to one-directional leadership are even more powerful.

Multi-directional leaders must be on guard against this path back to one-directional leadership and falling for errors they used to warn about. Remember that theological compromise usually doesn't start with a change of conviction. It doesn't start with abandoning biblical authority. It doesn't start with a new interpretation of biblical texts. It often starts with a feeling of solidarity with a new group. Our convictions, in other words, are formed not just cerebrally but communally.

And the danger for multi-directional leaders is that when our spirits are wounded, we're tempted to abandon the community that would hold us accountable and join a new crowd who would cheer us into compromise.

———

I hope this chapter has dispelled any notion that multi-directional leadership is about moderation, passivity, or a general squishiness when it comes to Christian belief and practice. Leaders who take this path will confront enormous challenges. The obstacles are major, though not insurmountable. Moving from a one-directional to multi-directional posture requires courage. We must acknowledge the personal pain associated with losing status among people whose respect we crave. We must also remain vigilant against temptations that would lead us to align with new allies against old friends.

The church needs fearless shepherds, full of wisdom and grace, who will challenge the political and theological tribalism that imprisons our imaginations. This fearlessness is impossible unless our fear of God and love for Jesus outstrip our fear of the bad trajectory or our love for ministerial acclaim. Thankfully, many faithful leaders have gone before us, men such as Charles Simeon, whose persevering faith was rooted in his commitment to the cross of Christ. As John Piper notes,

> Here is the root of Simeon's endurance: the cross of Christ giving rise to a "shuddering delight"—shuddering at his own remaining corruption that may betray his soul by fear of man and the love of the world; delight that rises higher than all that man can take or give, and therefore triumphs over all threats and allurements. Christ is all.[2]

This must be the heart of a multi-directional leader. Knowing our sinfulness and utter need for the One who is our wisdom (1 Cor. 1:30), we oppose the enemy of pride that would rob us of prophetic boldness. Our calling to provide faithful instruction must precede our desire to

2.   Piper, *21 Servants of Sovereign Joy*, 325.

preserve our influence. It matters more that we follow Jesus than that others follow us.

We must be so committed to proclaiming biblical truth that we're willing to defy any man-made category that would mute the beauty of the gospel or diminish our King's commands. Our faith in Jesus crucified and raised must foster a way of leading that is shaped by the cross, so that we're willing to lose earthly status for the eternal treasure of knowing the King and serving his people.

PART TWO

MULTI-DIRECTIONAL LEADERSHIP APPLIED

My goal in this section isn't to delve deeply into details of current evangelical disputes, much less offer a last word when it comes to particular debates. My aim is more modest—to introduce the idea of multi-directional leadership into these areas so that we grow in our discernment of dangers from multiple sides.

We'll look at one of the underlying factors for many debates: the proper posture of the church toward the world. Our optimism or pessimism regarding cultural change—and the extent to which we believe the culture is full of common grace or a place nearly devoid of useful knowledge and insight—matters for how we engage in various controversies.

Next, we'll look at three areas of current controversy among evangelicals. Two of these topics deal with public theology: the best way to address racial injustice, and the definition and extent of complementarianism. The third concerns the application of our theology when it comes to faithful Bible interpretation.

I realize heated debates and discussions change over the years—some of these challenges will fade and others will appear on the horizon. My goal with these examples is simply to show the multi-directional instinct at work, with the hope that these principles will assist church leaders in the future.

5

MULTI-DIRECTIONAL POSTURE

Debates regarding how best to relate to the world around us aren't new. Many of them flow from the beginning of the neo-evangelical movement, whose leaders sought to curb the isolationist excesses of a fundamentalist heritage *and* hold the line against encroaching liberalism. At the risk of oversimplification, let me briefly recount the history. Modernist theologians in the late 19th and early 20th century made experience the arbiter of truth and promoted "higher-critical" approaches to the Bible. This led traditional Christians in many denominations to reaffirm their commitment to the fundamentals of the faith and oppose rising preachers and theologians who downplayed or denied the Bible's testimony to supernatural occurrences such as the virgin birth of Jesus.

Many of the theologians and pastors most closely associated with the modernist perspective also shifted their concerns from the vertical to the horizontal (away from a gospel of personal salvation and toward political and social agendas that would improve society). In response, many fundamentalist leaders, fearing social activism would replace evangelistic passion, abandoned attempts at reforming societal structures or engaging in social ministry.[1] The fundamentalist–modernist controversy led to an unfortunate split between adhering to theological orthodoxy (the fundamentalists) and pressing for social reform (the modernists)—two aspects of Christian witness that, for earlier generations of evangelicals, had been kept together.[2]

CARL F. H. HENRY'S 'UNEASY CONSCIENCE'

By the late 1940s, some fundamentalists had an "uneasy conscience," the phrase Carl F. H. Henry used in a powerful little book that sought to rectify the problem of an increasingly isolated fundamentalism. "It remains a question whether one can be perpetually indifferent to the problems of social justice and international order, and develop a wholesome personal ethics," he wrote.[3] Personal righteousness and public righteousness should go together.[4]

Henry agreed with the fundamentalists who remained on guard against modernism and the social gospel, but he was convinced of dangers lurking elsewhere, which is why he warned that the fundamentalists who revolted against the social gospel "seemed also to revolt against the Christian social imperative," and that the fundamentalist

---

1. The history is a bit more complicated than this simple description. The *kinds* of social concern also underwent a bifurcation, with some fundamentalists becoming heavily engaged in social reform that opposed teaching evolution in public schools, and the consumption of alcohol.

2. The fundamentalists focused on five biblical concerns: the inspiration of Scripture, Jesus's virgin birth, his atoning death for our sins, his bodily resurrection, and the truthfulness of his miracles. For a brief overview of the fundamentalist movement and its influence on Protestantism and American society, see Thomas S. Kidd, *Who Is an Evangelical? The History of a Movement in Crisis* (New Haven, CT: Yale University Press, 2019), 51–73.

3. Carl F. H. Henry Jr., *The Uneasy Conscience of Modern Fundamentalism* (orig., 1847; Grand Rapids, MI: Wm. B. Eerdmans, 2003), 10.

4. This is a point that continues to be made by many in the wider evangelical tradition, including Vince Bacote, *The Political Disciple: A Theology of Public Life* (Grand Rapids, MI: Zondervan, 2015). Carl Ellis argues that biblical righteousness is a "four-paned window" composed of (1) piety and (2) justice, both (3) personal and (4) social. Pairing these dimensions in all possible combinations, we get four manifestations of righteousness: personal piety, social piety, personal justice, and social justice. Conversely, the "window of unrighteousness" is the photographic negative, characterized by (1) impiety and (2) oppression, both (3) individual and (4) institutional. Pairing these dimensions in all possible combinations, we get four manifestations of unrighteousness: individual impiety, institutional impiety, individual oppression, and institutional oppression. See Carl Ellis, "Biblical Righteousness Is a Four-Paned Window," The Gospel Coalition, www.thegospelcoalition.org/article/biblical-righteousness-four-paned-window.

movement "in the main fails to make relevant to the great moral problems in twentieth-century global living the implications of its redemptive message." He wrote,

> The ideal Hebrew or Christian society throbbed with challenge to the predominant culture of its generation, condemning with redemptive might the tolerated social evils, for the redemptive message was to light the world and salt the earth.[5]

Here we see multi-directional leadership at work in the nascent stages of the neo-evangelical movement. Henry, along with stalwarts like Billy Graham and Harold Ockenga (who in the foreword to Henry's book argued it was no solution for Christians to abandon "social fields to the secularist"[6]), pushed hard for reclaiming the social implications of the Christian faith.

Henry knew the dangers and pitfalls of modernist theology, and he knew how to fend off attacks against an incipient liberalism that would destroy the faith and deny the gospel. But he and other early leaders of the neo-evangelical movement felt uneasy because they saw fundamentalism's tendency to find its identity in protest. They knew the danger of groups that were perpetually at war, finding lesser distinguishing marks to battle over, cocooning themselves into ever-smaller enclaves of uniformity on the minutest doctrinal detail—while the rest of society was left to the influence of social activists whose churches had strayed from the gospel.

The consciences of traditional Christians became uneasy when they held up the fundamentalist movement to Scripture and noted the disparity. To deny the social implications of the gospel in order to avoid the dangers of liberalism would leave the flock vulnerable to wolves trying to establish Christian ethics apart from Christian orthodoxy, or to a quietist impulse that would rob the people of God of their saltiness. "A Christianity without a passion to turn the world upside down is not reflective of apostolic Christianity," Henry wrote.[7]

5. Henry, *The Uneasy Conscience of Modern Fundamentalism*, 30.
6. Harold Ockenga, foreword to Henry, *The Uneasy Conscience of Modern Fundamentalism*, xxi.
7. Henry, *The Uneasy Conscience of Modern Fundamentalism*, 16.

Some describe the early evangelical movement as a middle way between social-gospel liberalism and fundamentalist theology. I believe their method, though, more closely resembled that of Simeon, Stott, and other multi-directional leaders. They didn't seek to create a middle-of-the-road position between competing visions of Christianity, but to insist on two truths that should never have been separated: a commitment to the total truthfulness of the Bible *and* a passion for loving neighbor and seeing society transformed. Nowhere did they give the impression that we should compromise theological convictions in order to promote a social agenda, or temper our passion for the less fortunate by focusing more on theology. They saw the combination of word and deed in Scripture, and these leaders—in various ways and with different emphases—called Bible-believing Christians to both a high view of Scripture *and* concern for the world.

Leaders like Henry, Graham, and others were not infallible. While we applaud the multi-directional leadership that led them to reunite impulses that should never have been separated, we do find areas of their agenda deserve critique. (Some social evils, particularly those related to racial injustice, received inadequate attention. Although their approach was far better than that of fundamentalists like Billy Sunday, there was enough racial prejudice among their peers and funders to limit their pursuits in this area.[8]) My goal isn't to defend all aspects of their ministries or ignore areas where they fell short. I recount this history so we recognize the multi-directional sensibility in their vision and understand why debates about how best to relate to the world—avoiding the pitfalls of a fundamentalist obscurantism as well as the dangers of a social-activist liberalism—continue to shape the evangelical psyche today.

TIM KELLER'S 'CENTER CHURCH'

A more contemporary example of multi-directional leadership shows up in the ministry and outlook of Tim Keller, former pastor

---

8.   "The most conspicuous deficiency of the NAE (National Association of Evangelicals) was the failure of its white leaders to include African Americans and other nonwhites. Racial tension was also a major component in the evangelical crisis." Thomas S. Kidd, *Who Is An Evangelical?*, 76.

of Redeemer Presbyterian Church in New York City and co-founder of The Gospel Coalition. Keller's manual for "doing balanced, gospel-centered ministry in your city" is *Center Church*, a title that refers to several truths, one of which speaks directly to the aspiration of multi-directional leadership. The center is the place of balance, not compromise. He writes,

> We need to strike balances as Scripture does: of word and deed ministries; of challenging and affirming human culture; of cultural engagement and countercultural distinctiveness; of commitment to truth and generosity to others who don't share the same beliefs; of tradition and innovation in practice.[9]

Keller's version of multi-directional leadership relies on this idea of balance. I prefer terms like "versatility" or Churchill's image of "dexterity" (sometimes leaning heavily to one side and at other times to another, depending on the circumstances, in order to maintain consistency of purpose) instead of "balance," since the latter term could lead us to *equate* opposite dangers when the people we lead may be affected by just one. Still, this desire to remain faithful to *all* that Scripture teaches is key to multi-directional leadership.

What posture should we have toward the world? Keller writes,

> To reach people we must appreciate and adapt to their culture, but we must also challenge and confront it. This is based on the biblical teaching that all cultures have God's grace and natural revelation in them, yet they are also in rebellious idolatry. If we overadapt to a culture, we have accepted the culture's idols. If, however, we underadapt to a culture, we may have turned our own culture into an idol, an absolute. If we overadapt to a culture, we aren't able to change people because we are not calling them to change. If we underadapt to a culture, no one will be changed because no one will listen to us; we will be confusing, offensive, or simply unpersuasive. To the degree a ministry is overadapted or underadapted to a culture, it loses life-changing power.[10]

9.   Keller, *Center Church*, 16.
10.   Keller, *Center Church*, 18.

One could interpret Keller here as recommending a milquetoast, middle-of-the-road approach to cultural adaptation. But if the center of our ministry is the gospel, it becomes clear that Keller is not urging us to find a perfect place in the middle, but to uphold two vital passions at once: a rigorous commitment to maintaining the church's distinctiveness *and* a relentless reaching across cultural barriers with the gospel message. In this way, he echoes the warnings of previous evangelical leaders like Stott against the twin dangers of syncretism or obscurantism.

Keller lays out four models adopted by Christians who seek to faithfully bring the gospel to the world:

- The Transformationist Model "engages culture largely through an emphasis on Christians pursuing their vocations from a Christian worldview and thereby changing the culture. . . . Since the lordship of Christ should be brought to bear on *every* area of life—economics and business, government and politics, literature and art, journalism and the media, science and law and education—Christians should be laboring to transform culture, to (literally) change the world."[11]

- The Relevance Model is animated by the idea that "God's Spirit is at work in the culture to further his kingdom; therefore Christians should view culture as their ally and join with God to do good. The primary way to engage culture, then, is for the church to adapt to new realities and connect to what God is doing in the world."[12]

- The Counterculturalist Model places emphasis on "the church as a *contrast society* to the world. And while other models of cultural engagement speak about the important concept of the kingdom of God, this model strongly emphasizes that the kingdom is manifest primarily as a church community in *opposition* to the kingdom of this world."[13]

- The "Two Kingdoms Model" teaches that "God rules all of creation, but he does so in two distinct ways. First, there is the 'common

11.   Keller, *Center Church*, 210.
12.   Keller, *Center Church*, 219.
13.   Keller, *Center Church*, 224.

kingdom' established through the covenant with Noah in Genesis 9. . . . There is [also] the 'redemptive kingdom,' established with Abraham in Genesis 12. Only Christians are members of this kingdom, and they are ruled not through common grace and natural revelation but through the special revelation of God's Word."[14]

Keller believes each of these models captures something important about the relationship of the gospel to culture, but none, on its own, can give us the full picture.[15]

In assessing these models, he believes most concerns about culture can be summed up in two fundamental questions: "The first reveals our attitude toward cultural change: *Should we be pessimistic or optimistic about the possibility for cultural change?* The second question reveals our understanding of the nature of culture itself: *Is the culture redeemable and good, or fundamentally fallen?* Our answers to these questions reveal our alignment with biblical emphases as well as our imbalances."[16] Each model has a tendency, Keller finds, especially among its more strident proponents, to be either too optimistic or too pessimistic about cultural change.[17]

His point isn't that we should be true to all of these models at once, but that we should identify our current season, understand our ministry gifts and callings, and seek to incorporate the insights of the other models—all while avoiding the pitfalls associated with our preferred model.[18]

To return to our shepherding analogy, picture a field in the shape of a square, with four different sides, each representing one of the models Keller has described. Being multi-directional doesn't mean herding your sheep always to the middle of the field. It means you

---

14. Keller, *Center Church*, 231.

15. On a similar note, D. A. Carson, in surveying multiple approaches to Christ and culture as laid out in the influential work of H. Richard Niebuhr's *Christ and Culture* (New York: Harper and Brothers, 1951) concludes that each approach has a pivotal theme that is true but insufficient. D. A. Carson, *Christ and Culture Revisited* (Grand Rapids, MI: Wm. B. Eerdmans, 2008). For a broader examination of models for contextualization, see Stephen B. Bevans, *Models of Contextual Theology* (Maryknoll, NY: Orbis, 2013).

16. Keller, *Center Church*, 225.

17. Keller, *Center Church*, 225.

18. Keller, *Center Church*, 235–43.

know the side of the field where you and your flock reside. In communication with Christians who reside closer to other sides of the field, you seek insights that will benefit you, and you offer warnings and cautions that may benefit them. Multi-directional leaders don't seek a perfect balance; instead we lean into our ministry gifts and callings, understand the leanings of our sheep, remain aware of our cultural context, and stay alert to various dangers.

We've applied the concept of multi-directional leadership to the question of what posture we have toward the world, recognizing our strengths and weaknesses, tendencies and vulnerabilities. Now we turn to three areas of conflict within evangelicalism and consider ways multi-directional leadership can help us be faithful.

6

MULTI-DIRECTIONAL LEADERSHIP AND RACIAL INJUSTICE

The United States is embroiled in controversy over policing, racial prejudice, and injustice. While many agree regarding the need for reform in our criminal justice system and better police training, unity breaks down over the extent of racism in America, the definition of racism (is it primarily personal prejudice or structural in its manifestation?), right and wrong responses (protests, political action, riots, demands for solidarity?), and the best solutions (diversity training, anti-racist activism, colorblindness, affirmative action, reparations?).

I've noticed among church leaders a shift in recent years. On the one hand, many who once dismissed particular cases or sought alternate explanations when confronted with examples of police brutality have come to see a problem that needs to be addressed. Recent viral videos haven't made things worse, they say, but have more clearly revealed issues that our black and brown brothers and sisters have described from experience for a long time. A growing number of church leaders across the country recognize the persistence of racial discrimination, express their commitment to bringing a biblical perspective to bear on a subject fraught with political tension, and resolve to do something more than merely lament the state of society.

On the other hand, many Christians who've long been aware of the plight of many people of color in our society have observed shifts in the underlying philosophical foundations and ideologies among some of the movements driving change. Some leaders, while happy that more evangelicals are acknowledging the reality of continuing racial disparities and considering whether structural causes are at play, worry that loud secular voices are proposing solutions grounded in philosophies that contradict scriptural teaching. They're also concerned that identity politics and certain racial theories have become something of a substitute religion for their most enthusiastic adherents, a totalizing worldview complete with categories of law, judgment, heresy—a "gospel" of activism but without grace.

Multi-directional leadership can help us find the right path. If you're attuned to encroaching secular ideologies, you may be more alert to wolves preying on the sheep from one side of the field, but fail to see those sneaking up behind—those whose "right doctrine" in some areas makes it harder to spot their social apathy, racial prejudice, or ethnic nationalist mindset. Likewise, if you've come to see the devastation to the church's witness brought about by evangelical complicity in racism and injustice in the past, you may be alert to challenges from one side of the field but fail to see how revolutionary, anti-Christian ideologues are now moving in on your flock from behind you.

Multi-directional leadership will be necessary for the church to play a role in rooting out the evils of what the brother of Jesus condemns as "partiality" (James 2:1–13). We must come to grips not only with examples of racism in the present, but also the simplistic, whitewashed version of history that many of us have learned. Many white churchgoers today are surprised to discover the extent and depth of racist atrocities in American history and the lingering effects of injustice that became commonplace after the emancipation of slaves.[1]

---

1.   I often recommend Isabel Wilkerson's *The Warmth of Other Suns: The Epic Story of America's Great Migration* (New York: Vintage, 2011) because of the way it shows the depth of injustice during the Jim Crow era and its effect on the plight of African American families all over the country (not just the South), as well as the fortunes of their descendants in the years to come.

As Christians with a robust understanding of sin and injustice, we shouldn't be surprised by the ways that sinful attitudes affect structures in society, just as we're not surprised to see how laws promoting the sexual revolution help to create a culture where the unborn are seen as disposable. We shouldn't be surprised to see how easily hearts, turned against love for God and neighbor, continue to perpetuate injustice even when the laws on the books demand fair and equal treatment. We don't assume racism is only a generational sin that will pass away with our parents and grandparents. (A thriving online subculture of 20-somethings today promotes a social Darwinism that rivals the racism of eugenics-promoting intellectuals from a century ago.)

Many evangelicals today emphasize the importance of listening to people of color who open up about their experiences of injustice in our society, and rightly so. Empathy and mutual understanding will matter if we, as God's people, hope to share the beauty of the beloved community in a fractured world. Surely the church should be dissatisfied whenever we see the world's commitment to the flourishing of God-given diversity outstripping our own.

Further, Christians have a lot to learn from each other. Here is just one example: as white evangelicals begin to feel more out of step with mainstream society, especially because of our views of marriage and sexuality, what better place to turn than to the endurance of the black church through the centuries, led by brothers and sisters with experience in being a faithful presence in their community and with expertise in seeking change from the margins of society, not the center?[2]

2.   These are just a few resources that will benefit white evangelicals seeking to learn the history of and lessons from the black church tradition: Bruce L. Fields's chapter in *Five Views on the Church and Politics*, ed. Amy E. Black (Grand Rapids, MI: Zondervan, 2015); Thabiti Anyabwile, *Reviving the Black Church: A Call to Reclaim a Sacred Institution* (Nashville, TN: Broadman & Holman, 2015); C. Eric Lincoln and Lawrence Mamiya, *The Black Church in the African American Experience* (Durham, NC: Duke University Press, 1990); Eric C. Redmond, *Say It! Celebrating Expository Preaching in the African American Tradition* (Chicago, IL: Moody, 2020); Robert Smith, *Doctrine That Dances: Bringing Doctrinal Preaching and Teaching to Life* (Nashville, TN: Broadman and Holman, 2008). For a more academic reflection, see Mary Beth Swetnam Mathews, *Doctrine and Race: African American Evangelicals and Fundamentalism Between the Wars* (Tuscaloosa, AL: University of Alabama Press, 2018).

HISTORY, REFORM, AND REVOLUTION

It's good for church leaders to be alert to the reality and evil of racism in our society. But multi-directional leadership will not let us assume that every type of opposition to the evil of racism is *necessarily* righteous and good. For example, just as we must challenge a vision of history that whitewashes the past and valorizes people undeservedly, we also must confront revisionist attempts to tailor the past to fit within overly simple, materialist philosophies in which all the key individuals are placed in categories of oppressed or oppressor, or everyone is labeled racist or anti-racist based on contemporary definitions. Revisionist histories of this sort, instead of doing justice to the complexity of previous generations and showing them in all their complicated mix of vices and virtues, intend to delegitimize the American project altogether.

In *Orthodoxy*, Chesterton points out a problem with both the optimistic and the pessimistic perspective on history. The conservative tends to whitewash the past out of love for what has come before, but such love can become blindness, leading to the defense of the indefensible. "My country, right or wrong" isn't true patriotism; it's like saying "I love my mother, drunk or sober," when in reality the more you love your mother, the more you'd decry her drunkenness and want to see her sober. You have to love something enough to want to see it be the best it can be. The pessimist, on the other hand, takes a cynical view of history that fails to cultivate love or loyalty. It's one thing to reveal flaws in order to learn from the past and beautify the present; it's another thing to approach the past in a way that despises your history. In order to seek reform, Chesterton says, you have to love something enough to invest the time and energy into making it better.[3] The pessimist of today, however, often appeals to concepts and ideologies that would lead not to reform but revolution.

3.   For Chesterton, the proper approach to the world is to hate it and love it at the same time—to hate what needs changing and to love it enough to *want* to see it better. The proper response is a deep-seated patriotic loyalty to the world as good, alongside the realization that the world is fallen and requires reform. G. K. Chesterton, *Orthodoxy*, 119–46.

The civil-rights movement, at its best, was motivated by love for others, including white neighbors enslaved to their racial prejudice. The move toward justice stemmed from love, not hatred.[4] Multi-directional leadership means we will be alert to the conservative tendency to preserve a pristine but false view of the past that defends the indefensible *and* the revolutionary tendency to dismiss the world that preceded us and fall prey to hatred and disdain.

Multi-directional leadership means that we'll look to expose and eradicate racism, work for structural reforms that bring about real change, and charge churches to lead the way in pursuing harmony in society. We mustn't succumb to the counterfeit gospel of quietism that would tempt us to silence when God has called us to speak.

At the same time, multi-directional leadership should lead us to reject voices and proposals put forth by people who, while laudable in their stand against racism, have aligned with an agenda that is anti-Christian in both its root and aim. One of the major differences between the historical period of the 1960s and modern organizations like Black Lives Matter is the leadership of the church. This is why, on the one hand, Christians should be championing most loudly the theological truth behind the slogan "Black lives matter," especially in a culture that has routinely and regularly *devalued* black lives and bodies. It's also why, on the other hand, Christians should lament and oppose the anti-Christian and anti-family views of Black Lives Matter as an organization. It's possible, even if not popular, to do both.

Likewise, white Christian leaders are right to seek not only being *not racist* but also *anti-racist* in the sense of joining the cause of ending racial discrimination wherever it's found. But "anti-racist" can also carry the sense that authors such as Ibram Kendi give it, which assumes *any* inequity among people of different ethnic groups must stem from racism and would best be resolved by a Department of Anti-Racism looming over all policies and politicians at every level of society in order to enforce equality.[5] As other cultural commentators

---

4.   This is a key point made throughout Taylor Branch's magnificent trilogy, *America in the King Years* (New York: Simon and Schuster, 1988, 1999, 2006).

5.   Ibram X. Kendi, "Pass an Anti-Racist Constitutional Amendment," Politico, https://www.politico.com/interactives/2019/how-to-fix-politics-in-america/inequality/pass-an-anti-racist-constitutional-amendment.

have observed, only a totalitarian regime could pull that off, and not surprisingly, signs of soft totalitarianism (with the rise of cancel culture, and moments eerily reminiscent of China's Cultural Revolution's struggle sessions) have already appeared.[6]

THE EXAMPLE OF CARL ELLIS JR.

A black leader who has shown remarkable courage in both his decades-long activism in the fight for justice and his concerns regarding some contemporary solutions is Carl Ellis Jr., professor of theology and culture at Reformed Theological Seminary. In the introduction to the revised edition of Ellis's book *Free at Last? The Gospel in the African American Experience*, Amisho Baraka points out the ways in which Ellis models multi-directional leadership. As he writes,

> The prudence of a man or woman isn't measured by their ability to consolidate with every wave in popular thought, but how they rise above the wave in defense of a truth that transcends time.[7]

Baraka recognizes the dangers to the flock from opposing sides of the field:

> There are well-natured Black practitioners who were baptized into a one-sided orientation of White evangelicalism that was void of a biblical view in social justice. However, some Black practitioners who were educated in liberal institutions have a high regard for addressing systemic injustice but a low regard for biblical authority.[8]

---

6.   See Andrew Sullivan, "A Glimpse at the Intersectional Left's Political Endgame," *New York Magazine*, November 15, 2019, https://nymag.com/intelligencer/2019/11/andrew-sullivan-the-intersectional-lefts-political-endgame.html; and David Harsanyi, "Welcome to America's Cultural Revolution," *National Review*, June 9, 2020, https://www.nationalreview.com/2020/06/welcome-to-americas-cultural-revolution.

7.   Amisho Baraka, foreword to the signature edition of *Free at Last? The Gospel in the African American Experience* (Downers Grove, IL: InterVarsity Press, 2020), 1.

8.   Baraka, foreword, 2. Esau McCaulley describes the same two dangers in *Reading While Black: African American Biblical Interpretation as an Exercise in Hope* (Downers Grove, IL: InterVarsity Press, 2020), 6–16.

Baraka praises Ellis as someone who "refuses to be prostituted as a political pawn. He does not stand in a hopeless middle that hides behind indecision. He stands confident on the truth of God that refuses to auction off its allegiance. He may be too radical for some and not radical enough for others."[9]

Free at Last? doesn't moderate fidelity to Scripture or social concern. Ellis mines the depths of the African American experience and the rejection of "Slavemaster Christianity," celebrates the rich oral tradition in the black church, and describes the struggle for Christian ethics. The result is a beautiful picture of the black church's legacy and its contribution to theology, worship, and ethics. Over against a liberation theology that would deny essential Christian truths, he appeals to the black church's high view of Scripture and commitment to the gospel. Over against the failure of many conservative white Christians to translate their theological commitments into social concern, he lifts up the *both-and* approach to justice found in the black church.

As a multi-directional leader, Ellis also warns against ideologies that would lead to sinful partiality in various forms:

> Black is truly beautiful, but it is not beautiful as a god. As a god it is too small. . . . As an absolute, it will infect us with the kind of bigotry we've struggled against in others for centuries. . . . The Word of God embraced in the Black theological dynamic has always given us a transcendent reference point for reflection on ourselves and our situation. Whenever we seek to understand our situation without this transcendent reference point, we fail to find an answer to our crisis.[10]

More recently, Ellis has warned of parasitic forces that would co-opt peaceful protests for anarchy and revolution. Note how he speaks first to the danger on one side of the field (racism):

> In the last few years, we have had a laser-like focus on racism, and rightfully so, since it is a cancer in our society. It's a manifestation of human depravity, which is in itself the fatal disease of all mankind. . . . I reject

9. Baraka, foreword, 3.
10. Ellis, *Free at Last?*, 154.

the evils of racism, classism, and any form of dehumanization in all its iterations—they are all antithetical to the Gospel of Jesus Christ in which I believe, and are taught as an offense to God throughout the Scripture I hold dear.

Then note how Ellis switches direction to speak to another side of the field (opportunistic anarchy):

But . . . we must examine how anarchy is lying in wait to feed on our constitutional rights, and on our naiveté about our own vulnerability. . . . There is no love for humanity in the anarchist ideology; it is a nihilist's dream, manipulating the inclinations of non-anarchic nihilists like looters, and exploiting the rest of humanity merely as objects to be used, tossed aside, or crushed if they stand in the way.

The church, according to Ellis, must remain committed to "long-game discipleship" that looks beyond temporary protest strategies: "Not a discipleship into institutional, rote, shallow Christianity, but a discipleship into deep and practical biblical wisdom that affects every area of life—personal, cultural, and social."[11]

IMPORTANCE OF A BIBLICAL ANTHROPOLOGY

George Yancey, professor of sociology at Baylor University, is another example of multi-directional leadership in matters related to race. His *Beyond Racial Gridlock* lays out four secular models for dealing with racism, pointing out their appeal but also their dangers for Christians, before offering an approach of "mutual responsibility" grounded in Christian theology.[12] Yancey's work makes much of biblical anthropology. He understands how sin affects us all, and how the historically oppressed can become the oppressor, if given the chance. This is due to our sin nature. As Yancey explains:

11. Carl Ellis Jr., "Protest and Anarchy in Black and Blue," Prophets of Culture, June 4, 2020, http://drcarlellisjr.blogspot.com/2020/06/protest-and-anarchy-in-black-and-blue.html.
12. George Yancey, *Beyond Racial Gridlock: Embracing Mutual Responsibility* (Downers Grove, IL: InterVarsity Press, 2006).

We can understand why whites emphasize individualism while people of color emphasize structuralism. Our sin nature keeps us from recognizing our own shortcomings. Instead we focus on what others should do. The group that has benefited from the ravages of racism fails to recognize those ravages, since it would mean they must accept a level of accountability they do not want to accept. The groups who have been abused fail to recognize how things have gotten better and the fact that not all their problems can be blamed on racism. If we define racial problems in a way that does not include recognition of our sin nature, then we will have an incomplete definition and will be able to offer only incomplete answers.[13]

DISCERNMENT AND RACIAL JUSTICE

I realize that calling for multi-directional leadership in a moment like this opens one to criticism. *This is not the time to show dangers on different sides!* Not all dangers are equal, that's true. It's the history of white supremacy in our country that has left black people hanging from trees. And yet history also shows us how attempts to fight real injustice can lead to even greater injustice.

Nothing I've written here should mute the Christian leaders now finding their voice in these matters. My aim is simply this: to remind church leaders that the noble fight against racial discrimination will not be won by being intellectually indiscriminate—adopting any proposal or advocating any thinkers who may share a common diagnosis but have radically different goals or worldviews. Multi-directional leadership requires discernment, carefully sifting what is biblical from what is not, so that our unified action stands out with love in a world filled with disdain.

13. Yancey, *Beyond Racial Gridlock*, 26.

7

MULTI-DIRECTIONAL LEADERSHIP AND COMPLEMENTARIANISM

Let's take a brief look at sometimes heated discussions among those who refer to themselves as complementarians—a recent term defined in different ways by different leaders but that, at a minimum, refers to the conviction that the New Testament reserves the office of church elder for qualified men. I realize that some readers agree with this stance but don't find the label useful. Other readers may reject not just the label but also the position.

Among those who adhere to this position for exegetical, historical, and ecumenical reasons (it is, after all, the consensus view among Catholics, Orthodox, and most conservative Protestants today), debates over the meaning and significance of gender—and the extent to which gender distinctions matter for the Christian life—are ongoing in some evangelical circles. It isn't surprising we would find controversies on this topic. Recent gender theories that deconstruct the norms (and reality) of maleness and femaleness have been rapidly embraced by many culture-shapers in elite institutions.[1] Christians often feel beleaguered in society. We're concerned about trajectories within the church that might lead to the rejection of traditional Christian teaching on sex and gender.

What's more, among those who accept the term "complementarian" we find a variety of viewpoints on how best to apply this position in the church and at home. Additional descriptors have been added: "narrow" for complementarians who are "reluctant to say much more about the differences between men and women" beyond specific biblical texts, "broad" for complementarians who see a "larger theological 'vision' or 'definition' of manhood and womanhood that applies to all of life."[2] Other descriptions have risen: "soft" or "moderate" versus "strict" or "hardline" complementarianism.[3] There are complementarians who follow more closely the approach of John Piper and Wayne Grudem,[4] and some who better resemble that of Kathy Keller.[5]

The men and women who expressed their convictions in the 1988 Danvers Statement pushed back against views too closely aligned with secular, feminist ideologies that were making inroads in evangelical circles. They believed the Bible's teaching on gender difference matters for discipleship, so they sought to distinguish themselves from novel egalitarian interpretations of Scripture.[6] At the same time, the

---

1. For an overview of how the notions of gender and sex became separated and destabilized, see Carl R. Trueman, *The Rise and Triumph of the Modern Self: Cultural Amnesia, Expressive Individualism, and the Road to Sexual Revolution* (Wheaton, IL: Crossway, 2020).

2. Jonathan Leeman, "A Word of Empathy, Warning, and Counsel for 'Narrow' Complementarians," 9Marks, February 8, 2018, https://www.9marks.org/article/a-word-of-empathy-warning-and-counsel-for-narrow-complementarians

3. A good example of this distinction can be found in the essays and responses by Craig Blomberg and Thomas Schreiner—both complementarians, of different varieties—in *Two Views on Women in Ministry*, Counterpoints, rev. ed., ed. James R. Beck (Grand Rapids, MI: Zondervan Academic, 2010).

4. John Piper and Wayne Grudem, *50 Crucial Questions: An Overview of Central Concerns About Manhood and Womanhood* (Wheaton, IL: Crossway, 2016).

5. Kathy Keller, *Jesus, Justice, and Gender Roles: A Case for Gender Roles in Ministry* (Grand Rapids, MI: Zondervan, 2014).

6. For a number of essays from both perspectives, it may be helpful to read two books back to back: John Piper and Wayne Gruden, eds., *Recovering Biblical Manhood and Womanhood: A Response to Evangelical Feminism* (Wheaton, IL: Crossway Books, 2012) and Ronald W. Pierce and Rebecca Merrill Groothius, eds., *Discovering Biblical Equality: Complementarity without Hierarchy* (Downers Grove, IL: IVP Academic, 2005). Some books have sought to reframe the discussion,

coinage of the term "complementarian" indicates the desire to distance their views from an overly patriarchal perspective that shows up in many Christian writings over the centuries, including some of the most beloved church fathers. Even if the early complementarian leaders saw feminism as the primary danger threatening evangelicals, they recognized the dangers of an unbiblical patriarchy as well.

Fast-forward several decades. The culture has shifted in such a way as to destabilize gender altogether, to the point that traditional Christians find odd allies in certain feminists who, at least, recognize distinctions between men and women. Meanwhile, complementarians have continued to discuss and debate the appropriate application of gender distinctions in the home and in the church.

—

RECOGNIZING REACTIONARY TENDENCIES

Some of these debates stem from different interpretations of key biblical texts, but many react to problems surfacing in complementarian circles. For example, some churches tolerate (if not perpetuate) an environment that shrugs at misogynistic statements or fails to take seriously jokes that belittle women (whether in public or private). In some of the same groups, claims of sexual or physical abuse are dismissed or downplayed. Rigidly defined roles for men and women in the home and church can lead to extrabiblical rules, a legalistic spirit, and male and female stereotypes grounded more in cultural norms than in God's Word.

In reaction, other complementarians believe it best to focus not on "biblical manhood and womanhood" in distinction from the culture, but to stress male and female commonality in Christ. Little preaching or teaching explicates God's vision for male and female flourishing, except when critiquing the perceived excesses of stricter complementarian leaders. The danger seen and felt most in these circles is the incorrect application, or the failures and sins, of complementarians to their right.

such as Michelle Lee-Barnewall, *Neither Complementarian Nor Egalitarian: A Kingdom Corrective to the Evangelical Gender Debate* (Grand Rapids, MI: Baker Academic, 2016).

In reaction to churches who downplay their complementarian views, other complementarians then respond with warnings that—without clear articulation on what it means for God to make us male and female—we're in danger of losing our grip on the teaching of Scripture and succumbing to the cultural currents that would have us deny sex and gender altogether.

KNOWING YOUR FLOCK

How would multi-directional leadership apply to pastors committed to scriptural teaching on these matters?

As we saw in an earlier chapter, multi-directional leaders must know themselves and their flock. What danger is most likely to be prevalent among the people *you* lead? It's probably wise to assume that most young Bible readers begin with certain presuppositions about gender that are more in line with that of the culture. This means it won't be enough for pastors and leaders to merely stress *what* the Bible says about gender; they must also articulate *why* its vision for manhood and womanhood, sex, marriage, and authority in the church is good—for us and for the world. Don't let your concerns about the more troubling aspects of some complementarian churches keep you quiet about God's design. Unless we engage in careful, biblical teaching on sexuality, the family, and the church, we leave the flock vulnerable to cultural assumptions and unbiblical ideologies that mute God's glory in creating us male and female.

At the same time, multi-directional leaders must recognize the danger in overemphasizing gender difference; in denigrating women through words, actions, and attitudes; and in failing to pursue a healthy environment for all believers—men and women—to flourish in their God-given roles. Don't let your concern about a slippery slope toward cultural accommodation put you on a dangerous trajectory in the opposite direction. What if you remain unaware of ways you've fostered a culture that dismisses women's contributions to the church? What if your eagle-eyed vision of threats to complementarianism keeps you from seeing the dangers of misogyny, or blinds you to the absence of women flourishing in your congregation?

No matter where you come down on the specifics of complementarian debates, surely we should all offer unqualified denunciation of sexual abuse and domestic violence. In many cases, the church has failed at handling abuse allegations properly. The multi-directional leader must realize how easily a predator might misuse a sermon about marriage or authority in the church in order to manipulate his victims. It's true that abuse isn't only a complementarian issue—high-profile egalitarian pastors have been implicated in sexual assault and harassment—but surely those who believe in the protective aspects of male headship should be the loudest and most vociferous in exposing and denouncing any mistreatment of women and children.[7]

As a church leader, you must look at your congregation and discern to which side of the field your members are most prone to wander. Is the bigger threat in your context a flattening out of gender distinctions and a lack of trust in the goodness of the Bible's teaching? Or is it an overemphasis on gender distinctions that keeps the whole church from flourishing?

Staying attuned to your specific church is far better than merely reacting to social media, blog posts, or new books. The national conversation prompted by these debates is important, but the most important conversations are those that need to happen in your own context, as you seek to sound the right note at the right time.

---

7.   See Jonathan Leeman, "Why Complementarians Should Be 'First Responders' Against Abuse," 9Marks, March 25, 2020, https://www.9marks.org/article/why-complementarians-should-be-first-responders-against-abuse.

8

MULTI-DIRECTIONAL LEADERSHIP AND BIBLE INTERPRETATION

One more area of recent conversation among evangelicals combines hermeneutics, theology, and philosophy. What principles should guide our interpretation of the Bible? Does ethnic diversity matter when it comes to understanding the Bible? Should we consider a Bible commentator's background and experience? How do our cultural context and social location affect our interpretation of Scripture?

Some Christians believe we should seek to hear from diverse voices because it's all too easy for cultural blinders to distort our interpretation of Scripture or to screen out various elements of God's inspired Word that might challenge us. Other Christians worry that giving attention to an interpreter's ethnicity or experience leads us toward a relativistic mindset that minimizes the authority and sufficiency of God's Word. This is another area that calls for multi-directional leadership—the ability to recognize and oppose threats from multiple directions.

READING THE BIBLE WITH THE CHURCH

First, the desire to hear from different voices in other parts of the world merely extends a principle we believe to be true in our local church: *we read the Bible in community*. Rightly understood, the precious doctrines of the inerrancy, inspiration, and clarity of Scripture don't imply that hermeneutics is a solo discipline, something we undertake on our own apart from others' wisdom. We recognize the need for Christians to sharpen one another—to read and study Scripture together in the local church.

If we need the local church in order to interpret the Bible rightly, surely we also receive benefit when we listen to believers from other churches and cultures whose perspective might enhance our Scripture reading. To put it another way: we first adopt a principle—it's wise to study the Bible in community—and then we broaden its application. Just as Christians in church learn from one another, Christians from different cultures can do the same.

One of my favorite examples of how this principle works out in practice comes from theologian Mark Allan Powell. He writes about how Jesus's parable of the prodigal son is heard in Russia in contrast to the parable's reception in the United States. When recalling the story by memory, Russians are much more likely than Americans to mention the famine that precipitated the younger son's despair before returning home. Powell surmises that the siege of Leningrad—when the number of citizens who perished by starvation surpassed all U.S. and U.K. soldiers killed in World War II—remains within living memory of many grandparents and great-grandparents. That may be one reason why the famine plays a larger role to the Russian student who hears the parable.[1]

Evangelical scholars often stress the need to consider our social location as we approach the text, and many books seek to explain for Western readers ancient categories of kinship, patronage, honor, and shame. Certain community-based elements in the Old and New Testaments can seem strange or unintelligible to those of us raised in

1.   Mark Allan Powell, *What Do They Hear? Bridging the Gap Between Pulpit and Pew* (Nashville, TN: Abingdon Press, 2007), 13–18.

individualist cultures.[2] For the most part, evangelicals have celebrated these efforts and cheered the rise of theologians and scholars from across the world, whose cross-cultural conversations and commentaries answer our desire to better hear and heed the Scriptures. The goal, of course, is better Bible interpretation. This is why many Christians look to incorporate more global voices into their work—to diversify their reading lists in order to benefit from Bible readers whose social location and experience may challenge assumptions and preconceived notions we bring to the text.

RISE OF STANDPOINT THEORY

Some evangelicals, however, are reticent about these developments. They're concerned that the recent push to expand our horizons of biblical interpretation corresponds with trends in the academy and wider culture that question whether it's possible to genuinely understand the meaning of a text. Postmodern views of knowledge, meaning, and significance have given rise to "standpoint theory," described by Helen Pluckrose and James Lindsay in this way:

> Standpoint theory operates on two assumptions. One is that people occupying the same social positions, that is, identities—race, gender, sex, sexuality, ability, status, and so on—will have the same experiences of dominance and oppression and will, assuming they understand their own experiences correctly, interpret them in the same ways. From this follows the assumption that these experiences will provide them with a more authoritative and fuller picture. The other is that one's relative position within a social power dynamic dictates what one can and cannot know: thus the privileged are blinded by their privilege and the oppressed

2.   See E. Randolph Richards and Richard James, *Misreading Scripture with Individualist Eyes* (Downers Grove, IL: 2020). Consider also how Kenneth Bailey's excellent work on the parables, illuminated by his many years as a missionary in the Middle East, offers interpretive insight (even if in some cases he may lean too heavily on later traditions or contemporary Middle Eastern experiences). *Poet and Peasant and Through Peasant Eyes: A Literary-Cultural Approach to the Parables in Luke*, combined ed. (Grand Rapids, MI: Wm. B. Eerdmans, 1983).

possess a kind of double sight, in that they understand both the dominant position and the experience of being oppressed by it.[3]

In short, the more privileged a person is, the harder it is to understand reality. Privilege blinds. Applied to scriptural interpretation, this principle implicates many commentaries and theologians from Christian history (too many privileged white males) and casts a shadow of suspicion on even the most careful of exegetes, while favoring interpretive communities whose "lived experience" is oppression and poverty.

Unlike traditional evangelical hermeneutics, standpoint theory— when applied to Scripture interpretation—doesn't help us discover the meaning of the text, but instead destabilizes the idea of the text having a real meaning at all. Since no one can be perfectly objective in interpreting the Bible (because objectivity doesn't really exist), it's impossible to obtain true knowledge. Followed to its logical conclusion, standpoint theory leads to a conundrum: we are told our social location is so bound up in terms of privilege or oppression that interpretations from privileged groups are inescapably biased (in other words, wrong). But we are also told that the pursuit of a text's objective meaning is a pointless exercise, since all knowledge is culturally constructed. All that's left is *my* truth or *your* truth, and *our* truth is always bound up with and inseparable from our cultural perspective as interpreters. In the end, we're prisoners in a cultural cage; it's just that certain cages are better than others.

How does multi-directional leadership apply here? First, we must recognize two different dangers. Those who stress the importance of hearing from Christian interpreters from other parts of the world may slide toward some sort of standpoint theory that would cut them off from the wisdom of theological luminaries in the past. Those who stress their opposition to standpoint theory may fight postmodern problems with modern tools, cutting themselves off from the wisdom of diverse voices while minimizing the effect of the preunderstanding we all bring to the text. Multi-directional leaders must remain alert to both errors. How can we become better Bible readers who will not fall

---

3.   Helen Pluckrose and James Lindsay, *Cynical Theories: How Activist Scholarship Made Everything About Race, Gender, and Identity* (Durham, NC: Pitchstone Books, 2020), 194.

prey to philosophies (whether modern or postmodern) that undercut our commitment to the authority of God's Word?

DANGER OF MINIMIZING OUR SOCIAL LOCATION

Our first principle is to make sure we do not minimize areas of distance that affect our ability to understand the Bible. In *The Hermeneutical Spiral*, a standard evangelical textbook on how to interpret the Bible, Grant Osborne notes four areas of distance that challenge our ability to rightly understand God's Word: time, culture, geography, and language.[4] When we say we believe in the "perspicuity" or "clarity" of Scripture, we're affirming the truth that whatever is "necessary to be known, believed, and observed for salvation"[5] is clear enough that anyone, educated or uneducated, can read and study Scripture and come to sufficient understanding. But the doctrine of biblical clarity doesn't mean that all of the Bible is equally clear, or that the careful study of cultural, geographical, and linguistic differences is unnecessary.

Some Christians, in resisting standpoint theory or the idea that we should listen to voices from other cultures or backgrounds in order to better understand the Bible, may be tempted to minimize the effect of social location on our interpretation. It's easy to fall back into something like Scottish Common Sense Realism, which according to Osborne assumes that "the surface of the text is sufficient to produce meaning in and of itself. Therefore, the need for hermeneutical principles to bridge the cultural gap was ignored, and individualistic interpretations abounded."[6] We must be careful that we don't rightly oppose postmodern interpretive theories by championing modern and Enlightenment-era interpretive theories, which bring other problems.

Osborne urges us to consider the "effect of cultural heritage and worldview on interpretation. The sociology of knowledge recognizes the influence of societal values on all perceptions of reality. This is a critical factor in coming to grips with the place of preunderstanding

---

4. Grant Osborne, *The Hermeneutical Spiral: A Comprehensive Introduction to Biblical Interpretation* (Downers Grove, IL: IVP Academic, 2006).

5. Westminster Confession of Faith.

6. Osborne, *The Hermeneutical Spiral*, 27.

in the interpretive process."[7] No one comes to the biblical text as a blank slate. We bring certain questions and assumptions. It's important to interrogate our presuppositions so that we see how our preunderstanding may be affecting our Bible reading.[8]

DANGER OF EXAGGERATING OUR SOCIAL LOCATION

Someone might ask: does this mean that all interpretations of the Bible are culturally imprisoned? Does acknowledging preunderstanding make it impossible to arrive at a true and genuine understanding of the text? No. Multi-directional leaders acknowledge preunderstanding but don't fall prey to a postmodern exaggeration of the distance between us and the biblical text.

We can recognize the influence of culture on Bible interpretation without reducing all Bible interpretation to culture. The problem with postmodernism's influence on hermeneutics is that it reduces *everything* to culture. The hermeneutical task shifts from the universality of genuine knowledge to the context of the Bible reader.

Yes, we must recognize the effect of social location on our understanding of the Bible. Yes, we must acknowledge the benefit of dialogue with faithful Christians in other cultures so that we all come to a greater and more genuine understanding of the biblical text. Nevertheless, we should resist the notion that truth is contingent on one's point of view.

Richard Lints acknowledges the reality of preunderstanding:

All interpretation is shaped by the unique experiences of the interpreter. Part of this unique experience is the social location and cultural context

7. Osborne, *The Hermeneutical Spiral*, 505.
8. For example, Ajith Fernando explains several differences between a guilt/forgiveness paradigm and an honor/shame perspective. *Discipling in a Multicultural Word* (Wheaton, IL: Crossway, 2019). Another example is Esther Acolatse, whose book *Powers, Principalities, and the Spirit: Biblical Realism in Africa and the West* (Grand Rapids, MI: Wm. B. Eerdmans, 2018) shows that, whether we're in North America or the global South, we will tend to incorporate the biblical language about powers and principalities into frameworks or within worldviews that are foreign to Scripture. Enlightenment ideology affects North American readings, while dualism affects the global South. In seeking to interrogate our worldview, Acolatse offers a challenge both to Bible readers in the West and also to those in the global South.

of the interpreter. What one sees is influenced by what one is expecting to see. Those expectations in turn are formed in the complex interplay of individual and social orientations.[9]

But next he explains that this preunderstanding doesn't make a genuine understanding of the text impossible. Nor does acknowledging preunderstanding relativize all interpretations:

> This part of the cultural narrative appears to incline us to believe that all interpretations might be equally valid, or that one's interpretation should be insulated from criticism from other cultural locations. But the wider story into which our own particular narratives of human knowing occur point in the opposite direction. All interpretations are not created equal. There are better and worse culturally influenced readings.[10]

Lints is right. It's shortsighted to think that our interpretations are *only* enhanced when we engage Christians in other cultures. The truth is, all cultures are corrupted in some way or another. Yes, we can expect the readings of other Christians to expose some of our cultural idolatries, but Christians in other parts of the world should expect our interpretations to challenge their prevailing idols as well. This is one of the primary problems with appealing to lived experience as the standard by which all other interpretations must be judged. Multi-directional leaders see the threat in *both* postmodern theory *and* individualistic interpretations.[11]

One of the ways we can keep from exaggerating the distance between us and the biblical text is by recognizing and celebrating the widespread agreement we find with people who love Jesus and submit to his Word. D. A. Carson gives us a good example:

9.   Richard Lints, "To Whom Does the Text Belong?," in *The Enduring Authority of the Christian Scriptures*, ed. D. A. Carson (Grand Rapids, MI: Wm. B. Eerdmans, 2016), 927.

10. Lints, "To Whom Does the Text Belong?," 927.

11. "Traditional evangelical theology sometimes overlooks its cultural assumptions. But it is no solution simply to replace one culture's naïveté regarding biblical interpretation with a call to experience—as though experience were neutral—since experience always embeds theoretical commitments." David K. Clark, *To Know and Love God: Method for Theology* (Wheaton, IL: Crossway, 2003), 77.

When the *Africa Bible Commentary* was published a few years ago, its publishers and promoters kept insisting that at last we could hear the voices of Christians living in another continent reaching their own conclusions as to the meaning of Scripture, thus contributing to worldwide mutual Christian enrichment. In some measure, of course, this is wonderfully true. The *Africa Bible Commentary* devotes more attention than do Western one-volume Bible commentaries to exorcism, to questions surrounding ancestor worship, and to challenging the "health, wealth, and prosperity gospel." But what is most striking about the volume is that 90 or 95 percent of its content could be read and understood by, and could have been written by, believing Christians in virtually any part of the world. That should not surprise us: after all, we do share the same Book. Before we become too enamored with a narrowly conceived reader-response hermeneutic, we must ask ourselves in what ways the *Africa Bible Commentary* is not innovative, and shouldn't be.[12]

No one has all the truth, but we do have *truth*. Widespread agreement of Christians across the world and through the ages testifies to a common faith. Multi-directional leadership would have us remain alert to the dangers of underestimating *and* overestimating the function of social location in our ability to understand the Bible.

KNOWING THE WORD

In contrast to standpoint theory, we *can* know the meaning of Scripture. Carson recommends we distinguish between "genuine" and "omniscient" knowledge. Some Bible readers, rightly convinced by the postmodern critique of an Enlightenment-era certainty (an objective or God's-eye view of reality), assume that humility admits we can't really know anything. But this isn't true humility. Just because we can't know *everything* doesn't mean we can't know *anything*. We don't have to pursue omniscient knowledge in order to obtain genuine knowledge. You can know in part something true (genuine), even if you don't know that truth in full (omniscient). As Carson writes,

12.   D. A. Carson, "The Many Facets of the Current Discussion," in *The Enduring Authority of God's Word,* 12.

The Bible demonstrates, often implicitly but sometimes explicitly, that human beings can grow in knowledge, with appropriate certainty, responding to God's revelation with thought and active faith and obedient submission to our Maker and Redeemer.[13]

To deny the possibility of growing in knowledge, or to emphasize what we *can't* know, is to render God's revelation unintelligible. We give up on the possibility of obtaining genuine knowledge by appealing to humility, an excuse often conveniently employed to close our ears to what we don't want to receive from his Word.

A good example of the multi-directional instinct shows up in a document developed in Thailand in 2004 by a group associated with the global evangelical Lausanne Conference. The document points out how postmodernism is an ally for evangelicals only insofar as it exposes "the modern myths of exhaustive knowledge and human progress." Postmodernism has punctured Enlightenment hubris, and at this, evangelicals can rejoice. However, the Lausanne document continues, postmodernism "is radically sceptical about human ability to apprehend knowledge and regards the claim to possess knowledge as an attempt to gain power." For this reason, evangelicals must oppose standpoint theory. It's not because we wish to retreat to an Enlightenment fortress of absolute certainty, but because we believe "the Bible affirms our ability to know in part, even if not fully."[14]

READING THE BIBLE WITH HUMILITY

How, then, should we read? With epistemic humility—acknowledging our need for voices from other cultures and backgrounds, while maintaining humble confidence in the genuine knowledge we glean from Scripture as we read. We want to be humble interpreters of God's unchanging Word, relying on the Spirit to illuminate our understanding.

13.   D. A. Carson, "But That's Just Your Interpretation!" *Themelios* 44, no. 3 (December 2019), www.thegospelcoalition.org/themelios/article/but-thats-just-your-interpretation.

14.   Mark L. Y. Chan, "Following Jesus as the Truth: Postmodernity and Challenges of Relativism," *Evangelical Review of Theology* 31, no. 4 (October 2007), https://www.lausanne.org/content/lop/following-jesus-as-the-truth-postmodernity-and-challenges-of-relativism-lop-62-b.

What matters is a deep and abiding commitment to the authority of God's Word. To simply say "we need each other" is not enough, as some have used this truth as a tool for promoting passing fads or aberrant agendas that would have us stand over Scripture in judgment rather than kneel beneath it in submission. Carson is right to mention the indispensability of the Holy Spirit in this process:

> In the Bible's view of the relation between God and his people, we need the help of God's Holy Spirit to understand the truth as much as we need his help to do the truth. However that help may be mediated to us, the aim of thoughtful Christians, after all, is not so much to become masters of Scripture, but to be mastered by it, both for God's glory and his people's good.[15]

Likewise, David Clark reflects a multi-directional instinct as he sums up the need for evangelicals to avoid dangers in different directions.

> Two mistakes are possible. One is to pretend that cultural or philosophical preunderstanding does not exist or is relatively unimportant. This is where too much evangelical theology has failed in the past. . . . The other is to so delight in cultural and philosophical assumptions that they set in concrete the entire agenda for theology. This is where mainline/liberal versions of contextualization continue to stumble. Indeed, capitulating to contemporary agendas can lead to a faith that is indistinguishable from the surrounding culture. And if faith is indistinct from culture, it loses its vitality.[16]

Multi-directional leadership would lead us to intellectual humility—a way of reading Scripture that helps us avoid the pitfalls of both modernism and postmodernism. We want to bow the knee again and again before King Jesus, whose authority is exercised through his Word within the context of the beloved community for the benefit of every culture.

---

15.   D. A. Carson, *Collected Writings on Scripture* (Wheaton, IL: Crossway, 2010), 40.
16.   Clark, *To Know and Love God*, 78.

CONCLUSION

No leader can be perfectly multi-directional—always and equally aware of dangers from various points. And none of the leaders mentioned in this book is above critique. But we can glean wisdom from their example in how to lead with faithful versatility—a dexterity rooted in our commitment to truth.

Multi-directional leaders will often be unpopular. That's why we must relinquish the hope of pleasing everyone and reach instead for consistency of purpose—caring more about the voice of our Shepherd than our loudest cheerleaders or fiercest critics. Charles Spurgeon recommended his students have a "blind eye and a deaf ear" to various aspects of the church, especially the opinions and remarks made about the pastor:

> Public men must expect public criticism, and as the public cannot be regarded as infallible, public men may expect to be criticized in a way which is neither fair nor pleasant. . . . Too much consideration of what is said by our people, whether it be in praise or in depreciation, is not good for us. If we dwell on high with that "great Shepherd of the sheep" we shall care little for all the confused bleatings around us. . . . In proportion as praise pleases you censure will pain you.[1]

1.   Charles Spurgeon, *Lectures to My Students,* complete and unabridged ed. (Grand Rapids, MI: Zondervan Publishing House, 1954), 330–31.

Remember your calling. Care for the sheep you're called to shepherd. Focus on the community or organization in which your influence is most felt. Don't let the noise of the national news drown out the voices of the people you are responsible for. Love your church.

To young pastors, D. A. Carson and John Woodbridge write,

> Always remember that what endures after various movements come and go is the local church. At this stage in your life and ministry, do not worry too much about what is happening at the national level. Simply build the people to whom God has called you. Feed people the Word of God, pray for them, love them, convey the reality of God's presence to them by word and deed. What is important at the end of the day is the church—ordinary churches trying to live faithfully in a rapidly changing society. Ordinary churches pastored by ordinary people like you and me, knowing that we cannot do everything, but trying to do what we can and seeking God's face for his presence and blessing so that his dear Son might be honored and his people strengthened.[2]

This is the heart of a multi-directional pastor who guides people into faithful living amid culture changes and shifts. You'll face criticism for failing to toe the party line, for appearing inconsistent, for being too radical in one direction for some and too passive in another direction for others. But what greater honor do we have than to apply God's Word in our times for the good of God's people? What an adventure to remain alert to multifaceted dangers, to reject the middle way that slides into mushy moderation, to delight in truth's marvelous paradoxes, and to take on the prophetic mantle of speaking the right word in the right moment to the right people. And through it all, aware of our lingering sins and struggles, resting in Christ's mercy and relying on the Spirit's power, we lead with increasing anticipation of the day when we will hear from our Good Shepherd, "Well done."

Faithful versatility in protecting and shepherding the flock in a world of "many dangers, toils, and snares"—that is our ambition. God give us grace.

---

2.   D. A. Carson and John Woodbridge, *Letters Along the Way: A Novel of the Christian Life* (Wheaton, IL: Crossway, 1993), 226–27.

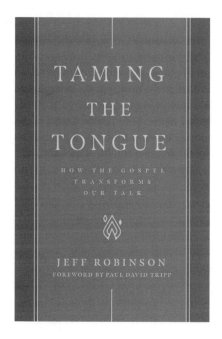

"This book hit home with me, perhaps because some of my greatest regrets have come from ways I've misused words—confidences I didn't keep, criticism I was too eager to offer, bragging to make myself seem important, dominating the conversation when I should have listened. I've also misused words by keeping silent when I should have come clean, when I should have offered praise, when I should have spoken up. These and many more insights on how we use our words are covered in this brief but wisdom-filled book—a great book to read prayerfully on your own, but even better to use to discuss with a small group."

NANCY GUTHRIE, author and Bible teacher

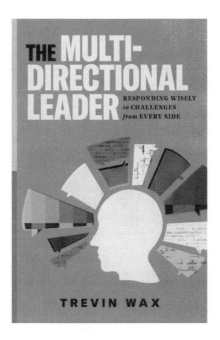

"Trevin Wax writes with keenness of insight, pastoral wisdom, and prophetic forcefulness. In this book he articulates the pressure today's Christian leaders feel from every direction. Wax remains one of my most reliable counselors for leading in a rapidly shifting context."

J. D. GREEAR, pastor, The Summit Church, Raleigh-Durham, North Carolina; president, Southern Baptist Convention

TGC THE GOSPEL COALITION

The Gospel Coalition (TGC) supports the church in making disciples of all nations, by providing gospel-centered resources that are trusted and timely, winsome and wise.

Guided by a Council of more than 40 pastors in the Reformed tradition, TGC seeks to advance gospel-centered ministry for the next generation by producing content (including articles, podcasts, videos, courses, and books) and convening leaders (including conferences, virtual events, training, and regional chapters).

In all of this we want to help Christians around the world better grasp the gospel of Jesus Christ and apply it to all of life in the 21st century. We want to offer biblical truth in an era of great confusion. We want to offer gospel-centered hope for the searching.

Join us by visiting TGC.org so you can be equipped to love God with all your heart, soul, mind, and strength, and to love your neighbor as yourself.